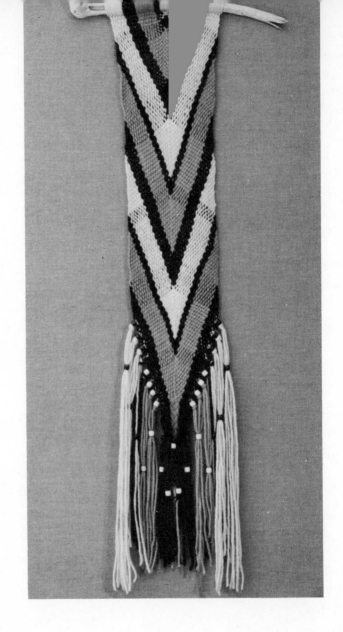

BY THE SAME AUTHOR

The Basic Book of

FINGERWEAVING

Esther Warner Dendel

WITH PHOTOGRAPHS AND DRAWINGS BY JO DENDEL

SIMON AND SCHUSTER · NEW YORK

SBN 671-21697-X
Library of Congress Catalog Card Number: 73-17697
Designed by Eve Metz
Manufactured in the United States of America

1 2 3 4 5 6 7 8 9 10

DEDICATION
For the members of the Denwar Crafts
Fellowship whose interest and enthu-
siasm made this book possible.

Table of Contents

6

7

Cornhusk figure with braided face by unknown American Indian [Collection of Blue Kiva Gallery].

How These Fingerweavings Grew

One of the many ways in which my years in Africa have enriched my life is that I began to see how delightful it is to *play* with string. In the hinterland villages of the rain forest, a spontaneous sense of play permeates everyday life. Playfulness has been one of the casualties of education and "progress" in the developing nations, just as in our own technological society.

In true play, a useful product is of small concern. The nagging questions, "How can I use this?" or "What do I *do* with it?" do not rear their practical heads to destroy the pure joy of rhythmic movement. In "braid cultures" a finger-woven article may be put to use but this is usually a secondary, almost accidental consideration. If an article is made intentionally for a practical purpose, its pattern will provide an outlet for the playful spirit.

In our culture, the use of an article, even an art object whose "use" is to match a sofa or fill a blank space on the wall, is of concern to a craftsman. In the desire to share the playful weaving techniques I learned in Africa and to interest others in trying them, I began to explore *what to do with them,* hoping that the simple pleasure of making something would surface as a by-product of the purposeful creation.

With this in mind, I set out to investigate the textile processes of many pre-industrial peoples—the ancient Peruvians, the Indian tribes of America, the Chinese. I began to think of contemporary uses for simple ways of handling fibers.

When I first presented these to our own group, the Denwar Crafts Fellowship, I met with varied responses. The more adventurous and imaginative—perhaps I should say the more playful among them—plunged in to see how the manipulations of making a tump-line or a dancing apron might work out usefully in our own society. As exciting products began to emerge, increasing numbers joined in the exploration.

The work spread beyond our immediate group through the efforts of Jean Hudson, who teaches in a retirement

THE BASIC BOOK OF FINGERWEAVING

community, and Celia Wagner, who organized a summer workshop for the young girls in her neighborhood. Through the enthusiasm of these two expert fingerweavers, people of all ages were caught up in the excitement of the work. Jean decided to try fingerweaving with a group of blind people with whom she does volunteer service. They received the idea with enthusiasm and are now doing beautiful braids.

Several craftsmen scattered about the country have been making experiments on their own. Françoise Grossen, a young Swiss girl now living in New York, does entire walls of braided rope. Being a master of design, she understands how to make powerful statements using simple braids.

We believe that the projects suggested in this book are only the beginning of what can be achieved with fingerweaving. All of us can enjoy expanding the possible.

Esther Warner Dendel

1 Working Arrangements, Materials, and Tools

Working Arrangements

In almost all fingerweaving the beginning ends are fastened in some way. There are a number of good working arrangements which accomplish this.

For narrow projects, such as belts, the beginning ends may be fastened under the clip of a clipboard. Or, ends may be gathered in a knot and placed just inside the drawer of a bureau. The worker backs away from the bureau as the woven piece lengthens under her fingers.

In the early days of French Canada, an awl was stuck in the wall and the yarns hung from it. The awl was pulled out and raised as the work lengthened. This method is still appropriate in camps and other places where a hole in the wall may not matter.

Pinning the work to a piece of building board is an excellent arrangement. Building board is sometimes called fiber board or insulation board. If you are not familiar with this material, ask the man at your favorite lumberyard to show it to you. If there are no scraps available and

you want to buy a large sheet, have it cut in rectangles of various sizes so you will have an assortment for a variety of projects. Bind the edges of each rectangle with masking tape to prevent the fiber from dusting off on clothing. Twelve inches is a good width for a bag or a small pillow.

Look around to find your own most convenient or available device. Joab Parker, an expert braider at age five, likes to tie yarn around the handle of his walnut rocking horse before he begins to work.

The length of the clamp depends on the width of the widest project for which it will be used. However, narrow projects *can* be done in a long clamp so it is best to make one large enough to do a variety of things. Thirty-two inches is a good length—long enough to hold the yarns for a poncho as well as for anything smaller.

The pieces of plywood are drilled an inch from each end to receive threaded bolts. A washer and wing nut over each bolt secures the boards tightly together.

If the clamp is more than 8 inches long, we drill holes and use threaded bolts and wing nuts every 6 inches.

Joab's sister, Kappie, ties a knot in the ends of the cords and holds them with her toes.

The Indians—America's first finger-weavers—usually drove a peg in the ground and tied their cords to that. For wider work they split a sapling length-wise, placed their strands between the halves, and tied it back together. Our own favorite way of working is a clamp, which is an adaptation of the Indians' split sapling.

Our clamps are made of two pieces of plywood, ¼ or ⅜ of an inch thick. A good width is 2½ inches.

A coat hanger may be bent into a hanging device for the clamp. As the work progresses, it is wound around the clamp. (*See opposite, top*)

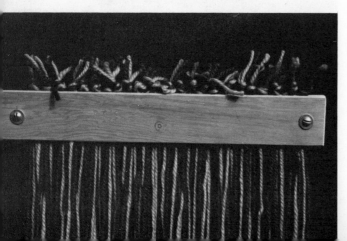

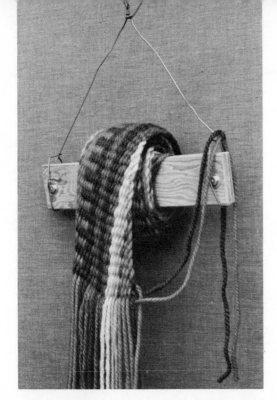

C-clamps it is likely to tilt forward, so the improvised wire hangers are really better.

Materials

Almost any cord pliable enough to be manipulated with the fingers may be used. Seine cord, jute, mason's line and other materials familiar to those who have done macramé are excellent for fingerweaving. Rug yarn and knitting yarn braid nicely. Chenille is good for texture. Fine yarns can be doubled or tripled and used as one strand. Some fingerweavers try to get several textures of the same color together before they

For big projects, we like to work over a piece of plywood set on an inexpensive easel, which can be folded away when not in use, the unfinished work left on it. You will find this a decorative, interesting piece in any room. Easels are convenient for other reasons. One may sit or stand to work because the height is adjustable. A square of ⅜-inch plywood, set on an easel, provides a flat place for the weaving to rest. One can gauge the tension of the work by comparing the edges to the straight sides of the board. Masking tape may be applied to the board to make a gauge for exact width. (*See right*)

The braiding clamp may be attached to the top of the plywood either with a C-clamp on each side or with wire hangers that can be made from coat hangers. If the braiding clamp rests on

begin, an assortment such as chenille, novelty yarn, knitting yarn, and rug yarn, all of which do not exactly match in color but which are similar.

Tools

Almost no tools are required. The essential tool in braiding has always been the human hand. Perhaps this is one of the reasons for the great satisfaction found in fingerweaving.

A crochet hook sometimes comes in handy and you will need a tape measure or a ruler to check the width of your work. T-pins (available at wig shops) are used if you pin to building board. Masking tape is useful in spacing yarns on a clamp. When these few items have been accumulated, you are ready to begin.

2 What to Make and How to Start

In preindustrial societies almost every item man needed was fingerwoven, from sandals to hats, from rat traps to fertility goddesses. Corn maidens or harvest dolls are made in England to this day, braided out of straw to mark the festive event of gathering in the grain and to ensure a good crop for the coming year.

Many books ranging from elaborate encyclopedias of rope work to scout manuals, weaving bulletins, and handbooks for fishermen deal with the subject of plaiting with the fingers. But very few of these show imaginative ways of using the techniques they depict. Lanyards made by scouts are usually destined to become key rings or whistle cords. Braids end up mounted on varnished boards, after which they are neglected or forgotten.

It is not our purpose in this book to show how to do all of the myriad braids and bands that have been known to man since prehistoric times, but rather to suggest ways in which contemporary craftsmen can make use of some of this ancient knowledge.

One idea has a way of leading to another and we believe that the ways in which our group of craftsmen have elaborated simple processes into beautiful objects opens up a whole new field of possibilities for all who wish to weave with their fingers.

Here is a list of a few of the things that we have created and that you may want to fingerweave:

Afghans
Bedspreads
Belts
Bolsters
Collars
Dress Trimmings
Dolls and Toys
Jackets
Halters
Hammocks and Swinging Chairs
Hand Puppets
Pillows
Plant Hangers
Pockets
Ponchos
Purses
Ruanas

Scarves
Sculptures
Shawls
Wall Hangings

Before one can follow the directions for any fingerweaving projects, a few terms must be understood. First of all, a working definition of braiding must be established.

When is a Braid a Braid?

Braiding means just what you probably think it does when you hear the word. If you picture a pigtail in your mind, seeing an interlacing of strands at an oblique angle, you are visualizing a braid made by braiding.

Curious as it may seem, not all braids are made by braiding. The noun, *braid,* means a narrow band. It may have been made by weaving, knotting, crocheting, looping—or by braiding. The verb, *braiding,* brings us back to what we do when we form a pigtail, although the pigtail is the simplest of all braided braids.

When weaving on a loom, one set of threads is clearly the foundation for the weaving. This set is called *warp.* Another separate set of threads is woven into the warp. This set is called *weft.* In braiding, these distinctions are blurred. A thread that has been functioning as a warp may become a weaving yarn and function for a space as a weft. In loom weaving, the wefts are usually at right angles to the warp. In braiding, the fibers tend to be interlaced at an oblique angle.

In general usage, *plaiting* and *braiding*

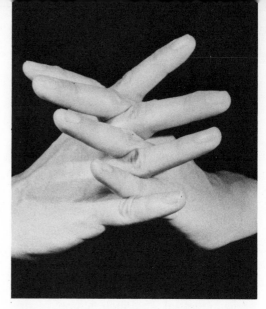

seem to be almost interchangeable. However, we will save the word *plaiting* for fabrics which are *interlinked* rather than *interlaced.* If you bend your little fingers and hook them together, this is the pattern of interlinking.

One word that must be defined before beginning to braid is *shed.* A shed is the passageway between warp threads when some are raised and some are lowered. In most fingerweaving, alternate threads are raised and lowered. One can understand the idea by placing the palms of the hands together and inserting the bent fingers between one another, forming a shed between fingers. In actual practice, every other yarn usually is thrown upward on the forefinger to form a shed.

Braiding is not to be confused with macramé, which is the art of knotting. We may use a half hitch knot now and then or mount a set of cords with larkshead knots, but our main concern is with ways of interlacing fibers with the fingers—in other words, *fingerweaving.*

To begin fingerweaving a narrow flat band such as a belt, all you need is some cord or yarn cut about one and a half times as long as you wish the finished belt to be, and a clipboard on which to secure the beginning ends. If the ends tend to pull free, tie an overhand knot in the end of each strand before placing it under the clip. Clips wider than those that ordinarily come on clipboards may be purchased at stationery stores and used over the edge of a piece of masonite cut as wide as necessary.

You probably know how to tie an overhand knot but you may not know it by that name. It is shown in the drawing.

Mounting Strands on a Holding Cord

In making cylindrical articles such as tote bags, pillows, and purses, a single or double cord, called a *holding* cord, may be tied around a piece of building board that has been cut to the width desired for the article. Two pieces of corrugated cardboard may be cut the right

size and glued together if building board is not available. The braiding cords are mounted on the holding cord all the way around the cardboard, front and back, after which the fingerweaving begins.

To mount a working strand on a holding cord, double it back on itself until the ends are together. This is called *doubling* or *middling*. Naturally, a middled cord must be cut twice as long as though single ends were going to be used. The loop at the middle is then slipped under the holding cord for an inch or so and the cut ends brought down through this loop. This knot is called a *larkshead* or a *price tag* knot.

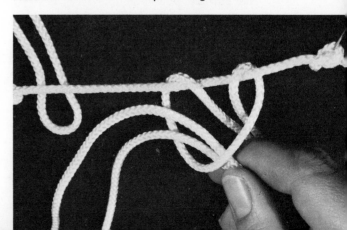

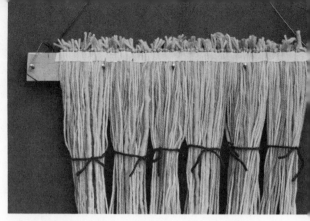

Seen head on, a little bar across each pair of ends is typical of the larkshead knot. If this seems distracting, remove the circle of mounted cords from the building board, turn it other side out, and slip it back on the board.

Starting to Work with the Yarns in a Clamp

To use the clamp described on page 12, remove the wing nuts and lay the bottom board of the clamp on a table or other flat surface, bolt ends up.

To secure the yarn in place, tie the cut yarns together in pairs with an overhand knot and place them over the clamp piece so the knots are just above the top edge. These knots prevent the

yarns from pulling out of the clamp after the work begins.

Once knots have been made and the pairs of yarns placed on the clamp, stick them down with short ends of masking tape. Masking tape keeps the yarns in order. It also enables the weaver to control the number of yarns grouped in each inch of space. Weave a small sample with the particular kind of yarn that is to be used, determining the specific number of yarns per inch in the sample. Mark off the bottom board of the clamp in one-inch units and place the desired number of yarns in each inch of space with tape. The tape is removed when the work is complete.

Usually the yarns pull together and the finished work is not as wide as originally visualized. For this reason, a small sample is recommended before any large undertaking is begun.

After the yarns are spaced out on the bottom bar of the clamp, set the top bar in place and tighten down the wing nuts.

As described earlier, the clamp, with the yarns in place, may be laid on a table top and worked there, or it may be hung. A coat hanger can be bent into a hanging device and suspended from a nail, hook, knob, or light fixture. If the hanger is wrapped with tape to prevent its scratching the furniture, it may even be hung from a high-backed chair. As the work progresses, the finished part may be wound around the clamp, as on page 13.

Naturally, to begin you will need only one of the several devices we have described. For a first project, most beginners start with a clipboard.

Four Categories of Flat Braiding

At first glance it may seem that the number of different kinds of braiding is endless. Actually, nearly all flat braids, regardless of size or pattern, fall into one of four basic categories. A more detailed chapter is included in this book covering each category more fully, but an introduction to them all will be helpful here.

In the first category, and probably the easiest to do, all of the cords move, one at a time, from only one outside edge to the other, weaving through all the other cords always in the same direction. The Peruvian flat braid is an outstanding example of this group. (*See top, right*)

In the second category of braiding, the outside cord on each edge weaves to the opposite side, weaving through all the cords. The shed is changed for the next row and all subsequent rows. Colored bands neither zig nor zag, but move in parallel lines. Stripes in a piece of work call for this technique, which will be more fully explained later.

In the third category of flat braids, the cords move from the outside edges to the center, first from one side and then from the other. The common pigtail braid is an example of this in its simplest form. When more strands are added to an edge-to-center braid, we have the French sennit. The outside cord on the left-hand side moves to the center and becomes the inside cord of the right-hand group. The outside cord from the

In the fourth category, the cords weave from the center to the edge, first to one side, then to the other. If an odd number of cords is used, it is the center cord that weaves to the right. If an even number of cords is used, the first cord at the left of center weaves to the right.

It follows then that the inside cord on the right is woven to the left.

The Osage braid is a special kind of center-to-edge braiding and Chapter 6 is devoted to how to do it and ways to use it.

These four basic rhythms are varied by the number of strands crossed and in changing from one category to another in the same project. Keeping the kinds of braiding in mind makes learning how to do them easier. We suggest that you start with the Peruvian flat braid if you are a beginning fingerweaver and move on to the other categories after your first project is complete.

right-hand side then weaves to the center and becomes the inside cord of the left-hand group.

3 The Peruvian Flat Braid

The Peruvian flat braid is one of the simplest and most versatile of all finger-weavings. Unlikely as it may seem until it has been tried, the weaving is done in only one direction. A warp at the outside right edge is led as a weft in an over-and-under sequence to the opposite side where it becomes a warp again, this time at the outside of the left edge. Left-handed persons may find it easier to weave from left to right.

The appearance of this braid varies considerably with the tension. If the strands acting as warps are pulled close together, they will cover the weaving strand completely. This type of weaving is called "warp face" and the effect is quite different than when all strands, warp and weft alike, are allowed to show equally, as shown here in a section of Peruvian braid.

This same fingerweaving was then tightened by pulling on each weft strand until it became a warp face weaving.

If the weaver wants the braid to have a warp face surface, the thread acting as weft is pulled snugly from edge to edge. This is done especially when a color pattern is specifically planned for being carried in the warp only, and the warps have been arranged in a given sequence at the start.

A belt is a good learning sample. The belt may be of one color and texture or

it may be of several colors and of several weights of yarn.

Jonda Friel likes to combine different weights of yarn. She will often use chenille with rug yarn, knitting yarn, and a fine novelty yarn which may have two strands used as one because of its small size. Her belt is in shocking pink, purple, orange, red orange, rust and gold. It is 66 inches long. Twenty strands of the various weight yarns described made a braid 1½ inches wide. Strands were cut 99 inches long, one and a half times the desired length of the finished belt.

For the sake of simplicity we show how to weave the Peruvian flat braid with only 6 cords instead of the 20 that Jonda used.

Step 1. Place the 6 ends of the yarn under the clip of a clipboard. Pick up the outside right strand and weave it to the left, over, under, over, under, over. It will extend beyond the work to the left.

Step 2. Pick up the next strand (now the outside right one) and weave it over, under, over, under, until it also extends beyond the work to the left—just below the first weft.

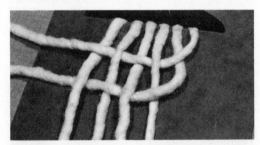

Step 3. Continue this rhythm. When the second weft emerges at the left, weave the first strand (the top one) down, under and over. This strand has now become a warp again and takes its place beside its fellow warps.

This is repeated for the length of the braid. The photographs show the strands

spread apart but they may be pulled together as tightly as one wishes.

As the braid progresses, the lower edge tends to slant from the right edge to the left. This is natural to this kind of braiding so do not worry about it.

The Peruvian flat braid is so simple and pleasant to do that we suggest you see what yarns you have around the house in colors that seem friendly together, regardless of their size, and start right in on a belt. Cut each yarn one and a half times the length you want your finished belt to be; if some of the yarns are quite fine, use 2 or even 3 strands as a single yarn. You may use as few or as many lengths as you wish, but the more you use the wider the belt will be. A clipboard or a piece of building board is the only equipment you need.

One of the most poetic hangings we have seen in Peruvian braid was made of seaweed by Joan Coverdale. The lengths were worked while they were damp; they stay in place after drying. They were loosely worked and each strand makes a delightful shadow pattern on the wall against which it is hung.

The delicate little floats, which grow on the seaweed, make a nice contrast to the linear quality of the stems.

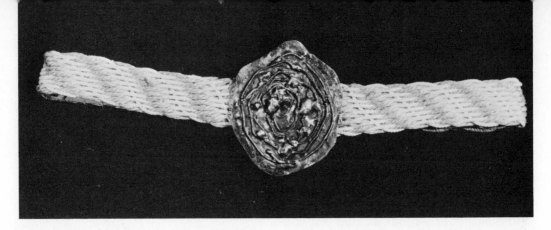

By alternating a strand of jute with a strand of seine cord when she set up her work, Irene Moog made a distinctive belt on which to wear a buckle handcrafted by her husband. The tension was worked so that the weaving strands show between the warps. The belt is lined with grosgrain ribbon to prevent stretching. After her belt was braided, Irene sewed across the ends with a sewing machine. Several rows of stitching kept the braiding strands firmly in place. She then bent the ends of the cords back and hid them beneath the ribbon lining. To attach the buckle she inserted the finished and lined belt beneath a bar on the back of the buckle, turned the end of the braid back on itself and stitched it in place by hand with matching sewing thread.

Dividing and Regrouping Strands

Much of the excitement in the Peruvian flat braid comes from the fact that it can be divided and later regrouped at any point along the way. Mary Jean Fowler used the braid to trim a detachable pocket, which she hand-loomed as a cylinder with a slit in the center for the hand opening. The braid decoration on the pocket progresses in the usual way until it is long enough to reach from the bottom of the pocket to the slit. It then divides into two smaller groups which are later subdivided and continued as pigtail braids. A length of braid interspersed with overhand knots is attached to the top of the pocket. This ties around the waist.

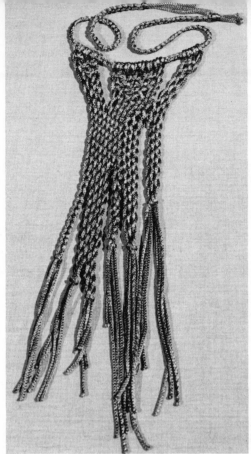

Kristin's hanging is the kind one wants to explore with the fingers, seeing the proportions of braids as they group, divide, regroup, and continue.

The ends of the hanging are finished in a variety of small braids. The top is a

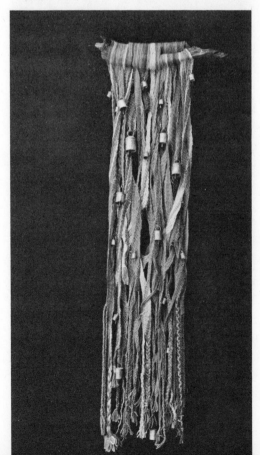

The Peruvian flat braid can begin as several separate braids and then be brought together as Jean Hudson did with rattail cord to make a necklace. In the beginning, the strands were hung from a length of round cord. A larkshead knot (shown at the beginning of the book) was used to mount the braiding cords, which were cut twice the needed length and middled. After weaving the groups separately for a space, Jean joined them into one unit and later divided them again.

Grouping, dividing, and regrouping of red, pink, orange and purple yarns created Kristin Levin's bright and beautiful wall hanging. (Color Plate #14).

25

piece of branched wood. Wrapping the branched area as well as the stem of the wood adds interest to the top and makes it an integral part of what happens below. The group of lighter yarns are well placed just out of center. Brass bells add to the gaiety of the hanging.

When one first learns a braid, the tendency is to work for even tension and a uniform width. In decorative pieces, the work is much more interesting if the tension and the width vary as they do in the wall hanging by Mary Jean Fowler.

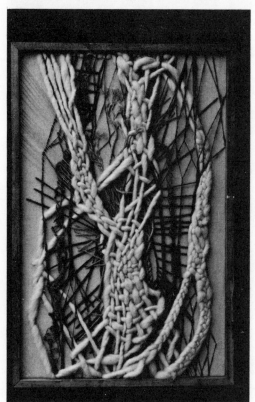

White strands of thick roving are fingerwoven, then separated, to meander

over the surface above random plaitings and stitchings of brown and natural fibers. These are mounted on coarse beige fabric and simply framed.

Patterns in the Peruvian Flat Braid

Patterns are established in the Peruvian flat braid by the order in which the colors are arranged in the beginning. One nice arrangement is to set up shades from dark to light, regardless of color. Jean Hudson shaded from red violet to gold to make her belt. A variation in Jean's belt is the braiding of individual yarns into simple pigtail braids for a short distance and then working the Peruvian braid with the pigtail braids, using each pigtail as though it were a single strand of yarn.

A chevron can be formed by braiding a pair of shaded bands, turning one of them over, then sewing the two bands together with the colors matching. The chevron shown in the photograph is a detail from a stunning bedspread finger-woven by Celia Wagner.

27

You will find the entire bedspread in the chapter on the Osage braid (Color Plate #15), but the same chevron effect can be achieved with two strips of Peruvian flat braid.

If colors are set up so that one dark yarn alternates with one light yarn, oblique bars are formed. If these go all the way across a braid, they give the effect of diagonal stripes.

Single dark yarns in a field of light create a pattern of darting streaks. Since

the dark yarn is in the lower shed, it appears on the upper surface of the warp every other time a weft is brought across, thus resembling a little running stitch skipping through the work.

One dark yarn with 2 light yarns on either side, surrounded by a field of medium color is an old Indian pattern.

Many Indian tribes of North and South America knew and used these and other patterns. Usually their end fringes were very long and braided into smaller groups, usually round braids of four strands as shown on page 94 in the chapter on square and round braids.

Two of the patterns described above are used in Kristin Levin's belt of orange, yellow and black.

AFGHAN IN PERUVIAN FLAT BRAID

Beginning fingerweavers are usually reluctant to start work on a wide project, much as they may wish an article of good size. One solution to this problem is to braid narrow bands and sew them together. For his project, Jo Dendel decided on an afghan made out of 4-inch strips of Peruvian flat braid. Heavy rug yarn was used in two shades of green, two shades of yellow, a bright orange and a magenta. The single strand of magenta skips along through the yellow as we have already described in patterns in the Peruvian flat braid. The orange and green make bars of color by being set up one green alternating with one orange.

Each strand was cut 10 feet long, yielding 61 inches of braid plus fringe. Starting at the left edge, the set-up is as follows: 5 moss green; 5 yellow green; 4 light yellow; 2 bright yellow; 1 magenta; 2 bright yellow; 6 red orange; 4 green and 4 orange alternating; 5 moss green; 5 yellow green—a total of 43 yarns. Ten of these strips were made.

The fingerwoven strips were sewed together lengthwise with a blunt needle

threaded with the moss green yarn. The sewing went under the edge yarn on one side, then under the corresponding edge yarn of the strip being joined. This makes a slight ridge and an interesting surface pattern. The finished afghan is 40 inches wide and 61 inches long plus fringe. (Color Plate #3).

The fringe at each end is 9½ inches long. It is braided in the 4-strand Indian round braid. (See the chapter on square and round braids).

4 Edge-to-Edge Weaving

When the outside cord is used as a weft, first on one side, then on the other, and both of the wefts move through all the warps first in one shed and then in another, the outside cords must be much longer than the others because most of the take-up occurs in these. Usually this type of fingerweaving is used when it is desirable for colors to move in parallel bands.

The two wefts, one coming from the right-hand edge and the other coming from the left-hand edge, may lie together in the same shed or the shed may be changed between each passing of weft. In our illustration, the two wefts lie in the same shed.

A PANEL TO WEAR OR HANG

Jonda Friel wove a panel that can be used as a wall hanging or worn as a long panel over a dress. The length is 37 inches. The cords are middled and hung from a wire neck ring. When the panel is used as a wall hanging, the neck ring is the hanger. When worn as an accessory, the panel hangs down the front of a dress, making a dramatic outfit out of any plain garment. (Color Plate #2).

Each of the four basic categories of flat braiding was used in this panel but it

#4—The poncho in linked French sennits, page 42

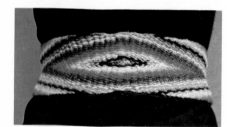

#6—The rainbow belt in Osage braiding, page 53

#7—A sleeveless jacket, page 78; Chinese Braids can be linked as they are woven.

#5—Jean Hudson's decorative collar, page 112

began with the one which is the subject of this chapter—the outside cord on each edge weaving alternately to the opposite edge.

When the yarns were mounted on the neck ring with larkshead knots, the colors were arranged so that each side was a mirror image of the other. Beginning at the center and working to the right, there was a pair of moss green thick and thin yarns. Next to them was a pair of red chenille yarns, followed by 3 pairs of brown yarns, 1 pair of turquoise, and 9 pairs of reds in various tones and textures including knitting yarn. The same number and colors of yarn were mounted left of the center. The yarns were cut 54 inches long (one and a half times the finished length) except for the two outside ones on either side. These were cut 74 inches long because of the amount of take-up that occurs when they are used over and over as wefts. The amount of take-up in this kind of weaving is in direct proportion to the width of the work and will vary from project to project.

When the center part of the finger-weaving had progressed 4 inches from the neck ring, Jonda mounted 4 pairs of moss green yarns on the ring on either side of the weaving she had just done. These yarns were woven down even with the center section using the Peruvian flat braid. This formed a braid about an inch wide on either side of the center weaving.

Jonda then began braiding all of the

yarns from the outside edge to the center including those which came from the Peruvian braids. She had moved into the third category of fingerweaving, the one we describe in Chapter 5 as edge-to-center braiding. The green yarns from the Peruvian braids were introduced, one at a time, into the total panel. No attempt was made to keep an even tension because Jonda wanted a point to be formed by the dark green yarns as they moved to the center area.

When all the dark green yarns had arrived in the center, Jonda changed to the fourth category of flat braiding and worked from the center to the edge.

A turquoise bead was attached at the point where center-to-edge braiding began.

It is important to say that no part of this panel was preplanned. Jonda assembled colors which picked up the scheme of a skirt she owned. The yarns were selected with variety of texture in mind. After the yarns were middled and mounted on the neck ring, the work went forward in a playful spirit, trying this and trying that. In the end each of the four major ways of braiding had been tried and they all worked.

#1—A pillow in Mexican dou[ble] woven as a cylinder, page 91

HANGING IN EDGE-TO-EDGE BRAIDING WITH SOME EDGE-TO-CENTER AREAS

Edge-to-edge braiding is usually used in combination with one of the other types of braiding. It is the way to keep stripes of color from moving in or out of the weaving. From a design standpoint, it gives stability to a composition. We can see it working in this way in another of Jonda Friel's wall hangings.

This hanging is 21 x 49 inches and is in earth colors. The color scheme was inspired by the driftwood stick, from which it is hung, and the rusty metal ring in the center. We see and enjoy off-white, soft golds, yellow ochres, taupe, and various grays. The fibers are a mixture of wool, cotton, rayon, novelty yarns, jute, and rayon chenille. The mixing of fibers to produce changes of texture is almost a hallmark of Jonda's work.

#2—A panel to wear or hang, page 30

#3—Jo Dendel's afghan, in the Peruvian flat braid

began with the one which is the subject of this chapter—the outside cord on each edge weaving alternately to the opposite edge.

When the yarns were mounted on the neck ring with larkshead knots, the colors were arranged so that each side was a mirror image of the other. Beginning at the center and working to the right, there was a pair of moss green thick and thin yarns. Next to them was a pair of red chenille yarns, followed by 3 pairs of brown yarns, 1 pair of turquoise, and 9 pairs of reds in various tones and textures including knitting yarn. The same number and colors of yarn were mounted left of the center. The yarns were cut 54 inches long (one and a half times the finished length) except for the two outside ones on either side. These were cut 74 inches long because of the amount of take-up that occurs when they are used over and over as wefts. The amount of take-up in this kind of weaving is in direct proportion to the width of the work and will vary from project to project.

When the center part of the finger-weaving had progressed 4 inches from the neck ring, Jonda mounted 4 pairs of moss green yarns on the ring on either side of the weaving she had just done. These yarns were woven down even with the center section using the Peruvian flat braid. This formed a braid about an inch wide on either side of the center weaving.

Jonda then began braiding all of the

yarns from the outside edge to the center including those which came from the Peruvian braids. She had moved into the third category of fingerweaving, the one we describe in Chapter 5 as edge-to-center braiding. The green yarns from the Peruvian braids were introduced, one at a time, into the total panel. No attempt was made to keep an even tension because Jonda wanted a point to be formed by the dark green yarns as they moved to the center area.

When all the dark green yarns had arrived in the center, Jonda changed to the fourth category of flat braiding and worked from the center to the edge.

A turquoise bead was attached at the point where center-to-edge braiding began.

It is important to say that no part of this panel was preplanned. Jonda assembled colors which picked up the scheme of a skirt she owned. The yarns were selected with variety of texture in mind. After the yarns were middled and mounted on the neck ring, the work went forward in a playful spirit, trying this and trying that. In the end each of the four major ways of braiding had been tried and they all worked.

HANGING IN EDGE-TO-EDGE BRAIDING WITH SOME EDGE-TO-CENTER AREAS

Edge-to-edge braiding is usually used in combination with one of the other types of braiding. It is the way to keep stripes of color from moving in or out of the weaving. From a design standpoint, it gives stability to a composition. We can see it working in this way in another of Jonda Friel's wall hangings.

This hanging is 21 x 49 inches and is in earth colors. The color scheme was inspired by the driftwood stick, from which it is hung, and the rusty metal ring in the center. We see and enjoy off-white, soft golds, yellow ochres, taupe, and various grays. The fibers are a mixture of wool, cotton, rayon, novelty yarns, jute, and rayon chenille. The mixing of fibers to produce changes of texture is almost a hallmark of Jonda's work.

#1—A pillow in Mexican double weaving, woven as a cylinder, page 91

#3—Jo Dendel's afghan, in the Peruvian flat braid, page 29

#2—A panel to wear or hang, page 30

#4—The poncho in linked French sennits, page 42

#5—Jean Hudson's decorative collar, page 112

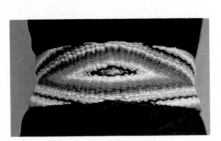

#6—The rainbow belt in Osage braiding, page 53

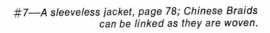

#7—A sleeveless jacket, page 78; Chinese Braids can be linked as they are woven.

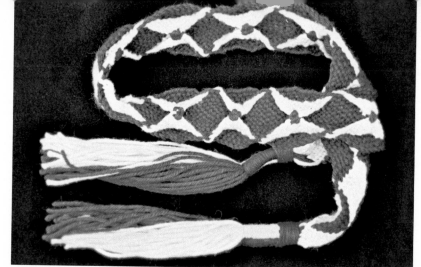

#8—A belt in Mexican double weaving, page 84

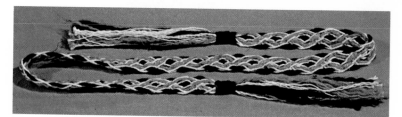

#9—A belt in the Chinese braid, page 74

#10—Man's tie, page 151. Any fingerweaving can be shaped for special purposes.

#11—The Osage doll, page 54

#12—The wall hanging begun in Mexican double weaving. Other fingerweaving techniques were added, page 86.

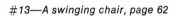
#13—A swinging chair, page 62

#14—A wall hanging in the Peruvian flat braid, page 25. Part of the fun of this technique is to divide and regroup strands.

#15—Celia Wagner's spectacular bedspread, page 65.

5 Edge-to-Center Weaving

Strands braided from the outside edges toward the center produce flat braids of surprising variety. Cords may be used singly or several cords may be used as one. The sequence may be over one and under one or it may vary. This way of working results in the common pigtail as well as in the more elaborate French sennit. Some of the small braids are introduced here, progressing to the French sennit and an explanation of how to widen it by weaving it together. First, the pigtail.

The Pigtail—Three Strands

Almost everyone knows how to braid a pigtail with three strands. The beginning ends are fastened (in the scalp, obviously, when working with hair); the working ends are free. There are many hairs in each strand. These are separated and kept in groups with the fingers. One at a time, each outside strand is brought inward over the center strand, first from one side, then from the other. Probably you can do this without thinking about it or even looking at it.

33

Four-Strand Braids—
the Chicken Tracks Braid

There are several ways to braid with four strands. The first one is much like the pigtail and even looks like it. If two of the four strands are dark and are placed in the center when starting the braid, a pattern is formed which is commonly known as "chicken tracks." You will see the reason for the name when you have braided it.

To start the braid, set up two dark cords together with a light cord on each side using T-pins or clipboard. Bring the light cord from the right-hand side over the first dark cord and to the left-hand pair of cords.

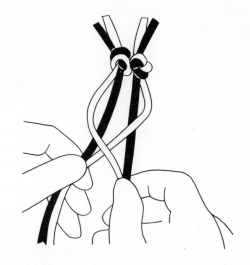

crossing two cords when you move in from the left.

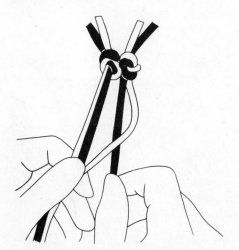

Now bring the left light cord over the left dark cord *and* over the the light cord which was brought to the center in the first movement of the braid.

You will always be crossing one cord when you move in toward the center from the right and you will always be

We have worked the braid in two tones of cord so you can see the chicken-track design.

Basic Technique for the French Sennit

The French sennit is a flat braid, usually with an odd number of strands that weave from the outside edges, alternately, to the center. It may be done with as few as 5 cords or it may involve many. Instructions are given here for using 7 strands but the process is the same for any number of strands providing they are an odd number. A slight variation provides for braiding with an even number of strands, which will be explained later.

Cut 7 ends one and a half times as long as the desired length of the finished braid. Place the ends in a clamp or pin them to a board. Four strands are grouped on the left-hand side, 3 on the right-hand side.

Step 2. Pick up the outside strand on the right-hand side and weave it over, under, over to the center where it will lie alongside the 3 strands on the left, making the fourth strand. It will be the inside cord of this group.

Step 1. Pick up the outside strand on the left. Lead it over, under, over to the center. Place it alongside the 3 strands at the right. It will lie on the inside of this group. There are now 4 strands on the right. Three remain on the left.

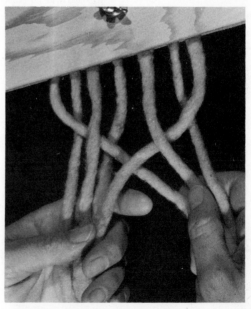

These two steps are repeated for the length of the work.

35

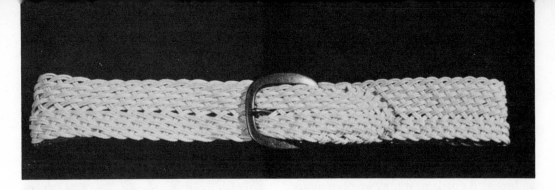

Using Several Strands as One in the French Sennit

Several strands may be braided as though they were a single cord, as in this man's belt by Doris Fox.

Doris used 2 strands as 1 in a French sennit. The belt is 40 inches long. Allowing one and a half times the length of the belt, or 60 inches, gave plenty of length for take-up and finishing the ends. However, since the cords were middled around the stem of the buckle, they needed to be cut twice 60 inches, or 120 inches long. The cords were grouped with 9 pairs on the left of the center and 8 pairs on the right of the center of the belt buckle. The tongue of the buckle separates the groups of middled strands. These 17 pairs of cords made a belt 2 inches wide using #21 seine cord.

In order to establish a shed close to the buckle, the first two rows of braiding were woven from the center out to the edge. After that, the braiding was done from the edge to the center.

Doris braided the length of the belt and then solved the problem of how to finish the braiding ends. The French sennit naturally tends to form a point in the process of weaving it.

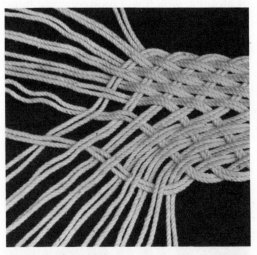

The cords from half the width are turned sharply to the back along a weft and become warps through which the other half of the cords are woven, a pair at a time.

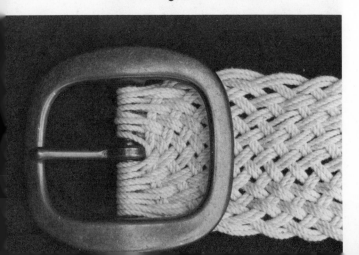

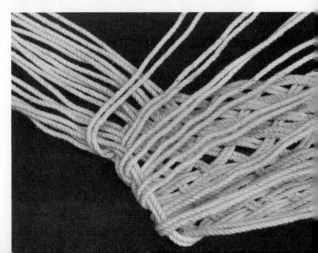

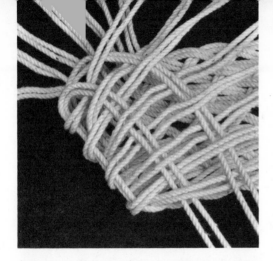

Each pair of ends projecting to the right is woven down to the left. These will later be pulled tight.

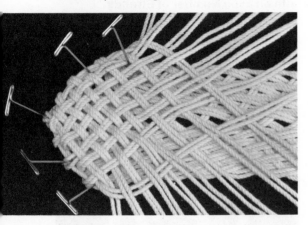

Before tightening the strands at the back of the belt the end point is pinned in place so that it will keep its shape.

Two rows of sewing machine stitching fasten the weaving securely before the loose ends are snipped off.

To make a wider belt, 3 lengths of seine cord may be used as though they were a single strand. Nine units of 3 cords each make an effective belt weave.

WORKING ON A HEROIC SCALE WITH ROPES

The internationally known young Swiss designer, Françoise Grossen, weaves enormous constructions with ropes, using simple braiding. Her "Blond Fish I" and "Blond Fish II" are 11 and 14 feet long, respectively. Each is 3 feet wide. "Blond Fish I" weighs approximately 40 pounds. (*See overleaf for photo*)

A detail from "Blond Fish I" shows the rhythm of the braiding. This one uses six units of three ropes each.

Large projects need to hang while they are being braided because the weight of the material itself helps maintain an even tension. Pulleys make a practical arrangement for raising and lowering the work when it is large and heavy. Françoise hangs the first rope on a pole which she raises as the work grows. She works standing and keeps the part she is working on at eye level.

Braiding from Edge to Center with an Even Number of Strands

Even numbers of strands may be braided similarly to odd numbers, starting at the outside and working to the center, except that if a strand starts on one side with an over-movement, the other side must begin with an under-movement to make the crossings come out in an under-and-over sequence at the center of the braid.

Changing the Over One, Under One Sequence

There are uncounted ways to vary the usual over one, under one sequence with either even or odd numbers of strands. For instance, there is a beautiful braid of 11 strands, which Celia Wagner made in various tones of yellow to place at the edge of the Osage braid in her bedspread (see page 66). She used several weights of yarn including a thick handspun Mexican one. (Color Plate #15)

To make this 11-strand braid, fasten the beginning ends under the clip of a clipboard or in a clamp. Allow an extra foot of length for every yard of finished braid. Hold 6 strands in the left hand and 5 in the right.

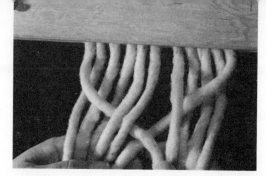

Step 2. Lift the outside right strand. Bring it over 3 strands and under 2 strands, then to the group in the left hand. It will be the inside cord on the left and does not cross any of the strands on that side.

These two steps are repeated for the length of the braid. The pattern emerges after several cycles.

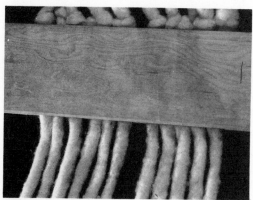

Step 1. Lift the outside left strand. Bring it over 3 cords, under 2 and so on to the other side where it becomes the inside strand of the group on the right.

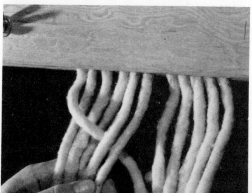

How to Link Sennits by
Weaving Them Together

If you bend your little fingers and hook them around one another you have an illustration of the technique of joining sennits by weaving them together. Set up as many units of yarns or cords as you wish in a braiding clamp. Each unit may consist of any odd number of yarns you find convenient to handle. This will depend partly upon the size of the yarn and partly upon the size of your hand. The yarns need to be one and a half times as long as the finished length plus a few extra inches for ease of manipulation during the last few inches of braiding.

Keep the yarns in groups to avoid confusion. To do this, encircle each half of each unit loosely with a length of yarn of contrasting color. For example, if you have 3 groups of yarn with 39 yarns in each group, the first encircling yarn will enclose 20 yarns, the next 19, thus organizing the first unit. The second and third units will be grouped similarly.

With the yarns in the braiding clamp and the encircling restraining yarns separating each half of each unit, the set-up is complete.

To begin weaving, refer back to the basic technique for the French sennit. A shed is formed in the left-hand half of the first unit by raising alternate yarns over the forefinger. The outside left yarn acts as the weft and is brought over and under the other yarns to the center. At the center it becomes the inside yarn of the second half of the unit and is placed in the restraining loop which encloses that group of yarns.

Now we move to the right-hand half of the first unit. A shed is made by raising the first yarn on the right and every other alternate yarn as far as the center. The first raised yarn on the right (the outside yarn of the group) becomes the weft and is brought to the left through the shed to the center.

When the weft from the right reaches the center, it becomes the inside member of the *left* half of the yarns and is placed in the restraining yarn which holds them. In other words, the wefts change positions from one half of the group to the other.

So far, the technique has been the basic French sennit in the first group of yarns. Now groups will be linked. Recalling the image of the locked little fingers, find the first yarn at the outside left side of the second group of yarns. Bring it through the space between the weft which has just been placed in the second half of the first group of yarns and the first warp which that weft transversed. A crochet hook is useful for bringing this yarn through the woven space. In the photograph, we have left the yarns widely spaced. In actual practice they would be pulled snugly together.

To summarize: the first yarn on the left-hand edge of the second group, the one which is going to be the first weft, is led over and under the adjacent weft in the second half of the first group. It then weaves to the center of its own group.

After the linking of the weft yarn, the second group is woven just like the first. If there are more than two groups, each successive group is linked and woven in the same way.

For clarity our photograph shows yarns loosely arranged. Two French sennits are linked in successive rows, weaving them together.

At the right edge of a flat piece of work, the outside right yarn has no other yarn with which to link. It just returns home to its own center. The weaving continues as described above, row after row, to the desired length.

It is easy to visualize this if you think about a straight line of people who hook elbows. The person on each end has no one with whom to link his outside elbow. If one were weaving sennits into a seamless cylinder for a pillow or bag, the set-up would resemble a *circle* of people in which everyone could link each of his elbows with a neighbor. To make a cylinder, work over a piece of cardboard or a piece of building board that has been cut the proper width for your project. Work around and around the board. This will enable you to adjust the tension and make a piece of work without bulges.

Tension is adjusted by pulling *down* on each yarn, one at a time. Usually it is not necessary to do this on every row. Five or six rows can be worked before equalizing any loose areas.

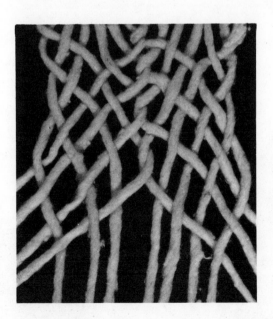

PONCHO IN LINKED FRENCH SENNITS—A SPECIAL PROJECT

Various tones and textures of gold and yellow yarns were used by Jo Dendel to make a poncho. Most of the yarn is rug yarn, but some of it is handspun Mexican yarn as thick as a little finger. The plan was to make a textural fabric of close color value. Part of the pleasure in viewing this work is being able to trace with the eye the path of the heavy cords as they make unequal V's across the width of the work. Shelley Spring, a fine young craftsman, models Jo's poncho. (Color Plate #4)

second half of the first group, and so on across the 3 groups.

The pattern uses two identical rectangles, each 21 x 40 inches. In the side view, the fringe at the back is where the end of one rectangle attaches to the side of the other.

Jo's first step was to decide how many yarns to use in each group and how many groups would be needed. Any odd number of yarns may be used as a group. Jo used 3 groups, each with 81 ends. This is too many for the average woman's hands. Four groups of 61 yarns would have been a better arrangement for me, and having 244 yarns instead of the 243 would have made no important difference in the width of the poncho.

Making the Set-Up for the Poncho

When the 243 yarns had been cut 67 inches long and placed in the braiding clamp, each half of each of the 3 groups was encircled with a length of yarn of contrasting color. There were 41 yarns in the first half of the first group, 40 in the

Beginning to Weave the Poncho in Linked French Sennits

Jo hung the braiding clamp in front of a piece of plywood set on an easel. Two strips of black masking tape on the plywood made a guide for the selvage. A total of 6 encircling yarns contains the alternating threads in each half of the 3 groups, explained in more detail below.

A shed was made in the first half of the first group by raising the alternate threads above the index finger. The first yarn at the left side of the left group becomes the first weft, but for convenience it is raised into the upper shed as the

shed is made. After the shed is made and this first weft is brought through it, the shed is changed, bringing all the yarns in the lower shed to the top layer. This holds the weft in place. After the shed is changed, a firm tug on each group of yarns packs the weft into the weaving.

An extra length of yarn is tied with a single knot to keep each shed separate. We now have a loosely tied restraining yarn around each half of each group of yarns and a snugly tied restraining yarn around the top shed of each half of each group.

The weft that has just come through the first shed is tucked into the restraining loop which contains the *second half* of the first group. It had 40 yarns before this visiting weft (which is now a warp again) made 41.

The right-hand half of the first group is now woven to the center and that weft

44

is placed in the restraining loop which holds the *first half* of the group.

This is the basic technique for the French sennit, except that the device of restraining loops has been added to keep all the cords in order. After the shed is changed, you will have woven the first row in the first group of 81 yarns. Continue across the other groups.

Completing the First Row of Weaving

A shed is made in the left-hand half of the second group of yarns by raising alternate yarns. The outside left yarn, which will become the weft, is raised and the second yarn is in the lower shed. *This weft yarn is linked with the first group before moving through the shed.* The tension is adjusted and the shed is changed and tied. The weft is placed in the restraining yarn which holds the second half of the second group. And the work continues, linking each group to the previous one.

Summary of Directions for a Poncho in Linked French Sennits

Two identical rectangles were braided. This summary reviews the steps in making one of the two rectangles.

The yarns were cut and grouped. Two hundred forty-three yarns, 67 inches long, were grouped in a braiding clamp in 3 groups, each group consisting of 41 yarns in the first half and 40 in the second half. Each half of each group was held in a restraining circle of yarn of a contrasting color.

First Half of the First Group

Step 1. A shed is made in the first half of the first group on the left-hand side with the first yarn on the left raised. Every other yarn is in the upper shed. Alternate yarns are in the lower shed.

Step 2. The first raised yarn at the left is brought through the shed as a weft.

Step 3. The weft is placed in the restraining circle for the *second* half of the first group where it becomes a warp again. (It has changed sides).

Step 4. The shed is changed and pulled tightly apart to pack the weft in place. The upper shed is tied with a length of contrasting yarn.

Weaving the Second Half of the First Group

Step 1. A shed is made in the second group. The first yarn on the right-hand side of the group will be raised into the upper shed. (After the shed is made it will become the weft to travel through the shed.) The second yarn from the right-hand edge goes in the lower shed, the next yarn up, and so on.

Step 2. The first yarn at the right-hand edge of the group is brought through the newly made shed to the left as far as the center of the group.

Step 3. The weft is placed in the restraining circle of the *left-hand* half of the group.

Step 4. The shed is changed and a yarn tied around the upper shed.

Weaving the Second Group
The second group is woven just like the first except that the first weft in the left half is linked through the first weft adjacent to it in the group that has just been woven.

Weaving the Third Group
The third group is woven just like the second. If there were more than three groups, the rhythm already established would simply continue.

Finishing the Poncho
Both ends of the two rectangles used for the poncho were finished with the Damascus edge (see page 121), using two yarns as one in making the knots. Had each yarn been knotted separately, the edge would have rippled because of the number of yarns per inch.

Sewing the Two Sections of the Poncho Together
When the weaving is completed there will be two identical rectangles that we will call Section 1 and Section 2.

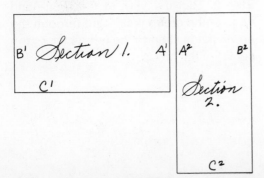

End A of Section 1 is slipped just under the side of the second section at A2 and sewed.

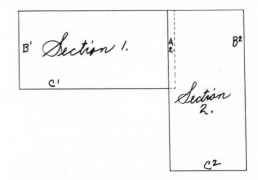

End B of Section 1 is folded over to B2 but *not* sewed.

End C2 is then brought just over the side of Section 1 at C1. This is sewed.

EDGE-TO-CENTER WEAVING

We used yellow yarn of the same kind used in the poncho itself and made small running stitches alongside the ridge of the Damascus edge to sew the two rectangles together.

Our photograph shows the completed poncho.

6 Center-to-Edge Weaving—
The Osage Indian Braid

The Osage braid is named for the Osage Indians, who used it extensively. Other tribes also knew this braid and in other books you may find the distinguishing chevron pattern attributed, correctly, to other groups as well. In calling it Osage, I am following the terminology of Mary Meigs Atwater, a noted weaving authority. *The braid is worked from the center to the outer edges.* Often there is a ridge down the middle of the length where two strands are crossed instead of one.

If the braiding begins at one end of the working strands and continues to the far end, all the chevrons will point in the same direction. If the braiding is begun in the middle of the *length* of the strands and braided first toward one end and then toward the other, there will be a diamond pattern in the center, and the chevrons will point in opposite directions on either side of the center diamond.

Two Ways to Manipulate the Strands

There are two ways to manipulate the work when doing the Osage braid. In one, the work is turned over each time after a weft passes from the center to the edge through the warps in the right-hand or in the left-hand half of the finger-weaving. In the other method the work is not turned from side to side. *Neither of these manipulations has anything to do with whether or not one starts weaving in the middle of the length of the yarns.*

The American Indians and the French Canadian women who wove sashes to trade to the Indians for furs *did* turn their work after each weft was brought from the center to the edge. They invented a braiding frame that is in use in Canada to this day and which makes it easy to swivel the work. However, for a simple learning project, the braid may swivel on a loop of string stuck under the clip of a clipboard. Our craftsmen are divided on the subject of whether to swivel or not to swivel. I like to turn my work because, when I do, I am at any given time working on the right-hand side. After an interruption, I find it easy to go back to where I was working before I was called away. But if one is working over a paper pattern or on a very large project, it is better not to swivel the weaving. For these reasons, we give directions for both ways of working.

Color Arrangement and Length of Cords

The yarns, usually an even number, are set up in color groups. The colors are arranged so that each side of the center is the mirror image of the other. The working yarns should be twice the finished length to allow for take-up.

OSAGE MUFFLER USING A CLAMP

A muffler of wool or acrylic yarn is a good beginning project for learning how to use the clamp. Determine the length of finished scarf and cut each yarn twice that length. Our first project was to be 3 feet long and about 5 inches wide when finished, so we cut 54 lengths of rug yarn, each 6 feet long. The colors are a medley of oranges and golds, varied but close to the same color value. The learning sample could be used as a belt instead of a muffler.

Use the clamp that has been described and pictured in the chapter on tools, materials, and working arrangements. The directions given involve turning the clamp and learning to begin in the middle of the lengths of the yarns.

Lift off the top board of the clamp and arrange the braiding yarns on the bottom board, *midpoint of the length of the yarn.* Place the clamp on a long table and place the yarns across it, one yarn at a time. Starting with the center bolt and working toward the right-hand edge of the clamp, place the yarns in sequence —4 orange, 4 gold, 4 orange, 4 gold, and 11 orange—a total of 27 yarns at the right of the center bolt.

At the left-hand side of the center bolt the same arrangement is made with the same number of yarns, this side being a mirror image of the right side. Fifty-four yarns now lie across the clamp at the halfway point of their length.

In actual practice the yarns are spaced about 10 to the inch but in this book they are spread apart to show each step. Illustrations show only the yarns below the edge of the clamp.

The top board of the clamp is set in place and the braiding begins. Three feet of yarn ends project from the bottom of the clamp for the immediate weaving. Three feet of yarn extend away from the clamp and above it. You will not be using these lengths for some time so gather them up into a couple of plastic bags to keep them from tangling or getting soiled while you work on the lower half.

Making the First Shed
in the Right Half

Step 1. I like to work on a table top. Other weavers prefer to hang their work and sit on a chair in front of it. The first step is to make a shed in the right-hand half of the yarns. The first yarn to the right of the center should go down. The second one should go up, and so on alternately to the outer edge of the row. It

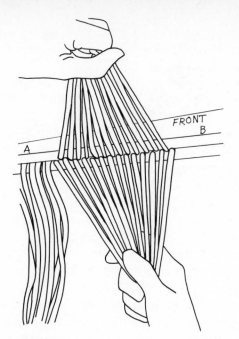

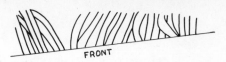

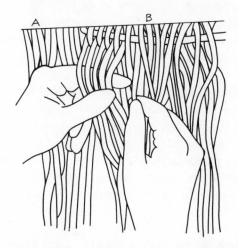

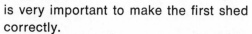

is very important to make the first shed correctly.

Step 2. The first yarn nearest the center in the left-hand group (side A) is brought through the right-hand shed already made on side B. It will project out to the right at right angles to the other yarns.

Step 3. Change sheds in order to keep the first weaving yarn in place. Everyone finds his own most comfortable system of changing sheds. I like to work from left to right, throwing the raised shed up on my index finger.

Step 4. Tie a slip knot in the new shed or tie it loosely with a short length of string.

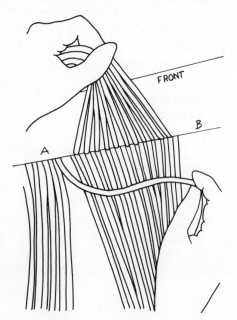

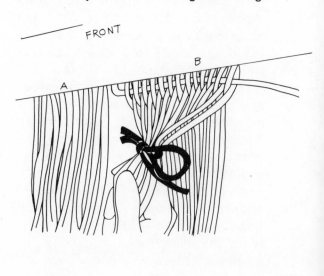

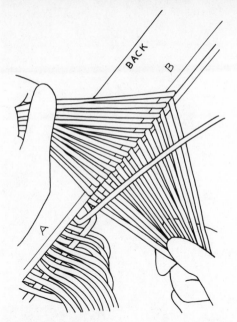

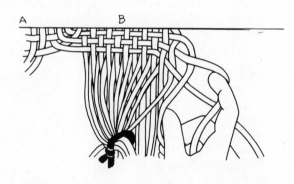

Step 5. *Turn the clamp over.* This brings the side we have labeled "Back" uppermost. The section that was just woven will now be on the left and the unwoven section becomes the right-hand side of the work. Make the first shed carefully, separating the lower and upper levels cleanly just as you did on the other side. The first yarn on the right of center goes into the lower shed. The first weft comes from the left of center. *

Step 6. Make a new shed to hold the weft in place. Tie it after it is completed.

Step 7. Continue weaving as described above and as soon as three wefts protrude at the right, weave the top one down, under and over the lower two wefts until it becomes a warp again at the outside edge.

Repeat the above steps, weaving a weft first through the right-hand half of the warps, then through the left-hand half. Because the clamp is turned after each passing of a weft, you will always be working on what at the moment is the right-hand half.

In the illustration, this fingerweaving has been spread apart somewhat at the center, so you can see the "over two" ridge which forms down the middle, where the working weft crosses over two warps.

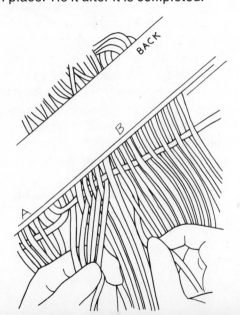

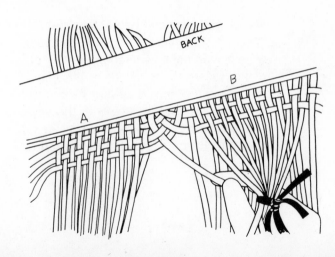

In actual practice, the two halves would be pulled snugly together.

As the weaving progresses, the edges tend to be lower than the center.

This slope is natural to this kind of braiding. At the finish of the fingerweaving, one may weave the center down until the end of the work has a straight edge. This is accomplished by stopping the weft short of the edge, yarn by yarn, in successive rows until the center is level with the outside edges. See the chapter on finishing techniques for drawings that show this leveling process.

Weaving the Second Half of the Piece

When the first half of the piece has been woven, take the unworked upper half out of the plastic bags. Remove the clamp and place the loose half in it as you did for the first half, this time with the edge of the woven half just barely protruding from the lower edge. Before tightening the clamp, be sure that the warps are equally divided on either side of the center.

The only difference in starting to weave the second half is that the clamp should be turned so that the side labeled "Back" is uppermost when the first shed is made. It will be easy to make the first shed because you will be able to see which yarns logically should go up and which should go down. The first weft is the yarn closest to the center on the left. It will make a right-angle turn when it is woven to the right.

The weaving continues as in the first half. Any of the methods described in the chapter on finishing techniques may be used to complete the work. If the tension needs to be adjusted, do this before the ends are finished.

The completed muffler is 5 inches wide.

The first Osage braid you weave is

52

likely to have a disconcerting pouch in the center diamond shape. This can be corrected without taking out the weaving. Pin the work to a flat piece of building board and place a row of pins along a straight line in the center. Some weavers use a board covered with squared-off fabric. (Printed straight lines do not always run parallel to the edge of the material, so a woven-in stripe is more reliable for blocking work.) After the center ridge of the braid has been pinned over a straight line, lift each weft, one at a time, with a crochet hook. Work the slack away from the center to the edge. This will form a series of loops along the outside edges. Again, one at a time, find the position of each weft after it has become a warp and pull the extra yarn to the ends of the weaving.

A RAINBOW BELT IN OSAGE BRAIDING

Jean Hudson used cotton rug yarn in spectrum colors for her rainbow belt. (Color Plate #6)

Cotton rug yarn is readily available in variety stores and from mail-order catalogues. The strands were cut 3 yards long. Twenty-six yarns make a belt wide enough to be dramatic. The colors were arranged so that each half was a mirror

image of the other. Braiding was begun in the middle of the length of the yarns to form the center diamond.

The way in which this weaving differs from the muffler is that the work was not turned after each passing of a weft. The right-hand half of the warps have a shed made with the first warp next to center in the lower shed just as with the muffler. However, on the *left* half of the work, the first warp next to center is in the *upper* shed. This produces the center "over two" ridge.

Jean wanted to narrow her belt at the back where it ties. To do this, toward the end she brought two wefts through a shed as though they were one yarn. One of this pair was then dropped at the back and later snipped off. It is a good idea to keep a record of how many yarns of each color are dropped so that the end of the second half of the belt can be shaped symmetrically. After being narrowed, the remaining ends of the belt were finished as Peruvian flat braids, which act as ties at the back of the belt.

LEARNING SAMPLE MADE INTO A DOLL

The learning sample need never be a waste of yarn. Joanne Onaga brought the two ends of her sample together, sewed the sides, and stuffed it. A pair of embroidered eyes, legs, and arms made an amusing doll. Legs and arms were wrapped, as on page 116. (Color Plate #11)

LEARNING SAMPLE
MADE INTO A COLLAR

Gertrude Loscar made her learning sample into a collar by attaching another sample-like braid to either side of the top of the first braid.

To make a collar similar to Gertrude's, you will need two colors of yarn, one light and one dark, a clipboard, a short length of heavy-duty string, and some beads.

For the center panel, cut 6 lengths of light yarn and 6 lengths of dark yarn, each 1½ yards long. Group the dark yarns on the left of the light ones.

Tie all the yarns into a bundle at midpoint of their length, using a separate piece of string. The ends of this string are placed under the clip of a clipboard so the work can swivel. The working set-up is pictured.

All the yarns are brought down together. This middles the yarn. There are now 24 ends, 12 dark ones in the center and 6 light ones on either side.

The weaving follows the same steps used in making the muffler, except that the beginning set-up is different. These are the steps:

Step 1. A shed is made in the right-hand half of the yarns. The weft that passes through this shed is the yarn closest to the center on the left. (Actually it is the other half of the first warp which was middled and placed next to center.)

Step 2. The shed is changed.

Step 3. The work is swiveled, flipping the warps which have a weft through them to the left-hand side.

Step 4. A shed is made in the unworked yarns and the first yarn on the left side, closest to center is brought through as a weft. The shed is changed.

Step 5. The work continues, turning it each time a weft has passed through half the warps.

The weaving is not pushed tightly to the top because the yarns at the very beginning will have other yarns fastened into them with larkshead knots. These will form the sides of the collar.

As the braiding approaches the ends of the yarn, you may stop the work at any place you wish. Gertrude wrapped all but the two outside yarns on either side. (See the chapter on finishing techniques.) She left these out of the wrapped bundle so she could string beads on them. An overhead knot between each bead spaces them.

Making the Side Panels of the Collar

To make the part of the collar that encircles the neck, cut 2 sets of light and dark yarns, each 1½ yards long. The number of yarns depends upon how wide a collar is desired and also upon how many yarns can conveniently be hung on the outside yarns at the top of the first panel. These yarns become an anchor cord or holding cord.

In the collar pictured we middled 4 light yarns, giving us 8 ends, and placed these in the center of the left side. On each side of the light yarns we middled 3 dark yarns, giving us 6 ends, for a total of 14 ends in all. These were attached to the outside yarn at the center panel with larkshead knots. This made one side of the collar. We set up the other side in the same way, with 7 yarns cut 1½ yards long and middled, giving us 14 ends.

After the sides of the collar are woven, the ends may be finished by any of the methods described in the chapter on finishing techniques. The collar may be fastened with snaps or with a short length of 4-strand round braid sewed to each half.

TOTE BAGS AND PURSES IN CENTER-TO-EDGE BRAIDING

Tote bags and purses are good projects for Osage fingerweaving. Helen Dickey found that her first attempt with the technique developed the pouch in the center that was mentioned earlier as a possible hazard. But instead of working the tension until it was even, Helen made use of the effect. The bottom of her tote bag slopes from each side toward the center. She cut the lining of the bag to fit the way the weaving developed naturally.

Sandra Crawley used red, orange and yellow rug yarn for her purse. She braided the center of each end of her work out level with the sides. (See the chapter on finishing techniques.) The top edges of the purse are held together with a short length of Chinese braid weighted with a stoneware circle and bead. The handle of the purse is in solid red Egyptian braid.

AN AMUSING SCARF IN CENTER-TO-EDGE BRAIDING

Jean Hudson added dash to her orange scarf by wrapping 14 inches of the center section. After this area was wrapped, it was doubled back on itself and connected by figure eight wrappings. The wrapping yarn is red orange and the scarf is a medley of oranges. We call Jean's headdress *Panache*.

WALL HANGINGS WOVEN FROM CENTER TO THE EDGE

Lisel Schmitt's wall hanging was begun by middling the yarns and hanging them on a piece of driftwood. Arranging the yarns on either side of the center Lisel worked out a pleasing proportion of light to dark. The chevrons all point the same way because the weaving was begun at one end and braided in one direction instead of at the middle of the length. Instead of braiding the end down level, Lisel grouped the naturally projecting wefts with overhand knots and beads at the edge of a dark chevron.

Eunice Ewing's wall hanging is much like Lisel's except that Eunice depended on the texture of her yarn for much of the effect. The ends are in Peruvian flat braiding. The material is a crinkley novelty yarn in blues and green.

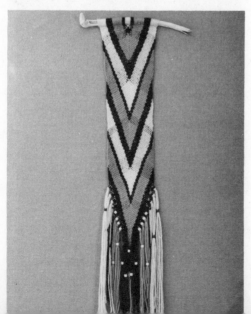

TWO CHAIRS IN OSAGE AND
PERUVIAN FLAT BRAIDING

Chair Braided on Frame of Steel Tubing

For her first braided chair, Doris Fox used seine cord, dyed in two tones of green. Pictured, young Ross Levin settles into the chair with his bear. It is also an extremely pleasant place to sit with a good book, and if one wishes to just sit, there are pockets on either side to store reading material neatly. Arm rests just above the pockets make for complete relaxation.

Twenty balls of #30 seine cord were required for the chair. The first step was to make the balls into skeins so the dye could penetrate the fibers. Doris dyed 3 skeins at a time. Each dyed batch of cords became progressively lighter in the dyeing process because the preceding batch absorbed and took out a certain amount of pigment. This produced a variety of tones and a medley of color values which was infinitely more interesting than flat, all-matching color.

A frame of stainless steel tubing was bent by Doris and her husband, Jerry, following a sketch she had made. Two identical pieces form the frame. It was taken to a welding shop after bending to make it permanently sturdy. If it is not possible to bend a frame oneself, it can be done at a machine shop if a pattern is supplied. The front and back are held together by a top and a bottom horizon-

tal bar on each side. This makes a sturdy frame.

The two pieces of the frame were welded together, and the steel tubing was completely wrapped with the dyed cord, around and around to cover the metal. The tops were wrapped together, and the steel ring from which they both hang was also wrapped. (Each braiding cord, after becoming a weft, is wrapped around the frame after it has crossed the warps, so the wrapping does not need to be as dense as one might think at the beginning of the work.)

A strand of wire was placed horizon-

59

spread the braiding cords apart to give a change of texture and do away with the necessity of adding a great many extra cords.

Near the top of the chair back, where fewer cords were needed, Doris dropped some of the wefts after wrapping each one around the frame. These were gathered into a big tassel and wrapped at the center back.

tally across the back on which to mount the braiding cords. Each strand was wrapped around the horizontal wire once and attached with an overhand knot. Thirty-eight strands, each 7 feet long, were mounted on the horizontal wire on each side of center, a total of 76 cords.

The back was braided in the regular Osage way except that each cord acting as a weft was wrapped once around the frame when it reached the outside edge before it dropped into place as a warp again. Each cord as it left the center was wrapped once around the warp, which would become the next weft. This gave added stability. As the girth of the chair increased toward the bottom, Doris

The sides of the chair are done in the Peruvian flat braid. Fifty-eight cords were used on each side, each cord 14 feet long. After each cord was middled, it was 7 feet long. There were 116 ends at the beginning of the braiding. These were hung on the horizontal bar at the top of the chair. The braiding was done in the usual manner of the Peruvian flat braid except that each cord was wrapped around the frame before it started across the warps as a weft cord. It was also wrapped around the frame after it came across the warps. It then hung down and became, once again, a warp.

To compensate for the increasing width of the chair as it approached the bottom, extra strands were middled and added. These were attached by dropping at midpoint of the length over the weft in the previous row. (See the chapter on widening, narrowing and shaping.) In any fingerweaving, if a *pair* of strands is added, the over and under sequence is not disturbed.

The lighter cord, which does not extend the entire length of the chair, shows how smoothly new strands weave into the work.

In the back panel, spreading the cords apart made a decorative accent and eliminated the addition of a great number of strands.

The cords at the bottom were gathered up under the seat and another tassel was made there. This tassel conceals a brass bell which tinkles merrily but gently when the chair is swinging. (*See above*)

The chair is a delight whether swinging or quiet, whether one is in it looking out or out of it looking in.

A Swinging Chair with a Rope Frame
After Doris finished her first chair, she began thinking about alternative braided chairs which might be made without stainless steel frames. The new chair she designed has rope supports. A piece of exterior plywood spreads the ropes at the top and at the bottom. Little Laura Whelan enjoys the completed chair. (*See page overleaf*) (Color Plate #13)

61

Doris' first step was to dye 14 balls of #30 seine cord and 24 feet of hemp rope. The rope and some cords were dyed orange, other cords bright yellow, and the rest canary yellow. Before dyeing, the balls of cord were made into skeins, one skein to a ball—to do this the cord is wrapped around a board or two chair backs and then tied lightly together. The skeins were washed in soapy water, then rinsed in clear water to prepare them for the dye. Skeins should drip

dry because if they are placed in a dryer they tend to tangle.

After the cord and rope were dyed, 2 pieces of external plywood were cut. The one for the top is 10 x 12 inches and the seat is 12 x 18 inches. The plywood is ¾ of an inch thick. The corners were rounded with a rough file and then sanded. A ½-inch hole was drilled in each corner of each piece, ¾ of an inch from the edge. The seat, the top, and a metal ring (3½ inches) were painted bright orange. (*See opposite, top*)

Doris saved the leftover dye, so in case she ran out of cord she would be able to color a new batch. But as it turned out, she did not have to use this precautionary measure.

With the material assembled and prepared for use, Doris was ready to begin. The hemp rope was cut in two sections, each 12 feet long. Each end was wrapped very tightly with plastic tape to make sure it would not spread and to make it easy to thread through the holes in the boards.

The 2 ropes were run through the metal ring and middled, giving 4 ends. The 2 ends of the first rope were brought through the holes in the front of the boards and the 2 ends of the other rope were brought through the holes in the backs of the boards. The height of the boards was then adjusted. The top board was slid down until it was about 7 inches below the metal ring. The front of the bottom board was adjusted at 35 inches from the top board but the back edge

was lowered another inch to give a comfortable "sitting slope" to the board. To keep the boards in place, each rope was wrapped with some cord of matching orange just below the hole in the board through which it was strung. A cord about 7 inches long was used for this wrapping. (See the chapter on finishing techniques.)

The wrapped area increased the diameter of the rope so the boards could not slip down.

With the top and the bottom boards in permanent place, a holding cord 36 inches long was tied from the front to the back of the right side, across the back of the chair, and across the left side. The holding cord is 9 inches below the top board.

The braiding cords were then cut and tied on the holding cord with an overhand knot. The cords are 8 feet long. There are 66 on each side of the chair

and 44 on each half of the back, a total of 220 cords. To keep them from tangling, the cords not being used at the time were placed in plastic bags.

The cords were arranged in color groups in the back so that each half was the mirror image of the other. Various color groupings were used at the sides of the chair. Almost any arrangement of colors would be effective. By alternating one yellow with one orange cord in some of the areas, bars of color were formed during the braiding. (See the chapter on the Peruvian flat braid to understand how to produce pattern in this braid.)

It was necessary to pin the edges of the braid to a piece of building board during the braiding process to maintain the correct width and tension. The Osage braid was used for the back of the chair. It was braided to the top board in 28 rows and the braiding continued above

the top board for 12 rows. The regular Osage braid was used, except that each weft cord was knotted around the rope with an overhand knot when it reached the edge.

After the cords above the holding cord had been woven to the top, the ends below the holding cord were woven down to the bottom board both at the back and the sides. When they reached the bottom board, the cords were separated into smaller groups and the braiding continued in the Peruvian flat braid to bring the strands underneath the bottom board of the chair. Each group was then wrapped and brought to a center tassel.

The cords from the sides of the chair were also grouped and wrapped under the bottom board and fed into the tassel.

The top of the chair was finished by

wrapping groups of cords for a space, then combining groups and wrapping until all the loose cords on each side and the back had been gathered into large ropelike wrapped strands and brought together above the top board in a gay

tassel tucked inside (see page 62).

At the center back of the chair, Doris accentuated the center of the diamond shape, which is typical of the Osage braid, by pulling it out to a point and tying a bell on the tip.

BEDSPREAD IN OSAGE AND OTHER BRAIDS

Of all the articles we could imagine doing in fingerweaving, a spread for a king-size bed seemed to offer the greatest challenge—a challenge Celia Wagner was willing to accept. At the time, we did not know the greatest width to which it is practical to braid. Using heavy rug yarn, we decided that the central panel might be 44 inches wide. A French sennit of 41 strands and two widths of Peruvian flat braid of 38 strands each on either

side of the center panel plus four narrow, textured strips of bright yellow filled out the spread to the width of the bed, which is 72 inches. The 44-inch center panel proved to be entirely manageable. Celia says that if she does another bedspread, she will do the entire top in one seamless piece! (Color Plate #15)

The yarns for the center panel were arranged on the bottom bar of the clamp, eight to the inch. With the heavy rug

yarn, this density allows the yarn acting as weft to show slightly. Celia suggests that a denser braid would be firmer and another time she would use more strands per inch and braid more tightly.

The colors in the Osage-braided, 44-inch center panel are bright red orange, orange, pumpkin, gold and bright yellow. They are arranged in groups on either side of the center of bright red orange.

The handsome brass bed for which this spread was made has a 24-inch drop so the spread had to be 124 inches long. Twice the finished length is needed for the Osage braid but a little more gives

a margin of safety. The 352 yarns needed for the 44-inch center panel were cut 248 inches long. The diamond shape, typical of the Osage braid, began a little below the center of the length in order not to conflict with the pillow area at the top. The yarns were arranged across the bottom bar of a braiding clamp with about a foot more of their length above the bar than below it. The yarns above the bar were gathered into plastic bags since they were not to be used until the bottom half of the length had been completed. The clamp was too large to turn handily so Celia did the Osage braid without turning the work in the way which has already been described in the chapter on the Osage braid.

In the bedspread, as in any Osage braiding, the working edge tends to slant from the center toward the outside edges.

In some projects, the edge would need to be braided down level. In this case, Celia finished the ends, color group by color group, with the Peruvian flat braid that started on each side with the slope already present. The Peruvian flat braids cascade to the floor.

When the bottom half of the center panel had been completed, the clamp was turned so the unbraided yarns issued from the lower edge. The yarns for above the bar were removed from the plastic bags and the top half of the center panel was woven. When the lightest color value reached the center area, the weaving continued, color group by color group, in Peruvian flat braids matching those at the bottom of the spread.

The unlinked braids were assembled by tacking them to a gold sheet. At the joining seam, 6 lengths of flat-sided Kru Coast braid give a neat ridge and an accent of moss green color.

The skirt on either side of the bed repeats the kinds and colors of braids used on the top, except for the Osage. Two Peruvian flat braids sewed together create the chevron pattern usually associated with the Osage braid. This could have been done as one Osage braid rather than in a pair of Peruvian braids.

67

One of the most delightful textures in the bedspread is found in the narrow bright yellow bands at the edges of the Osage center panel and at the edges of the bed. It is an 11-strand patterned braid described in the chapter on edge-to-center braiding. Very heavy handspun Mexican yarn was combined with rug yarn in slightly different tones of bright yellow. This narrow band gives a tailored look to the edges.

Basting in green running stitches down the large center panel to the sheet below carries the green color to the center of the spread, and the brass headboard gleams beautifully with the reds and golds. The whole ensemble is poetry in fingerweaving.

Ten pounds of finest quality yarns were used in the spread. It is color fast, moth proofed, and it cost $75.00 to make.

We would not recommend a king-size bedspread as a beginning project. But an experienced fingerweaver should not be intimidated by the idea. Fewer obstacles were encountered than we had anticipated and the challenge of a really important piece of work kept Celia interested and totally involved. The end product is incredibly beautiful.

SPECIAL PROJECT IN OSAGE BRAIDING—A RUANA

A ruana is a graceful garment that has reached our country from South America. It is something like a poncho and something like a shawl but different from either. To imagine it, think of a long rectangle of woolen fabric about 52 inches long and 40 inches wide, cut down the center lengthwise a little more than half

way, as shown in the newspaper pattern.

Imagine that you are placing the end which is not cut over your left shoulder, the two cut ends extending to the right. The narrow strip at the back is brought forward over the right shoulder and hangs down in front. The narrow strip at the front is flipped back, although either the back or the front may be thrown over the shoulder first.

The ruana may also be worn with the wide part hanging down the back and the two narrower panels in front but it seems less dashing that way. It is a comfortable, casual garment that keeps the neck and shoulders warm while the arms swing free.

Mel Kernahan has done our special project, a fingerwoven ruana, in purple, blue, turquoise, green, and chartreuse heavy rug yarn.

Two matching panels, with the typical Osage diamond in each, were later laced together with a yarn-threaded needle for 23 inches of their length. The lacing together of the two panels was done by taking a threaded needle under one yarn at the edge of one panel, then under a corresponding yarn at the edge of the other panel.

Each yarn was cut 96 inches long, allowing half the length for take-up. Mel says that if she were doing another ruana she would cut each yarn about 20 inches longer, for a total of 116 inches. There are 168 yarns in each panel but the number would vary according to the kind of yarn used. A little experimenting with the yarn of your choice will determine how many yarns per inch should be allowed. Each of Mel's panels is 20 inches wide.

Interesting proportion was achieved by varying the number of yarns in each color group. On either side of the purple, which forms the center diamond shape, there are 6 green yarns followed by 14 blue. Each successive color group has a

different number of yarns but whatever number is used on one side of the center is repeated on the other side of center in each panel. Part of the fun of making a ruana is working out proportions of colors that please you as you lay them out on the bottom half of the braiding clamp.

After the beginning section is woven from the clamp almost to the ends of the yarns, the clamp is moved up on the weaving and the other end is woven—

just as described in the directions for the Osage braid on page 52.

The ends of the panels were finished with the Damascus edge. Directions for this are given in the chapter on finishing techniques.

Placement of the diamond in an osage ruana is a matter of personal choice.

Mel placed her diamond nearer the end that was to be sewed to the second panel so it would appear as a complete motif.

It is quite possible to weave the chevrons all in one direction, by starting at one end rather than in the central area, but this gives the weaver longer ends to handle and does away with the diamond pattern.

A ruana seems to us to be one of the most practical and handsome projects for fingerweaving. Mel chose the Osage braid because of the opportunity it gives for patterned color. Other braids might have been selected, especially the Chinese. Narrow braids can be sewed together to form a ruana, in which case the French sennit would be a good choice. However, more experienced fingerweavers might prefer weaving a wide web rather than sewing narrow strips together.

7 The Chinese Braid

Chinese braid produces a striking pattern and is one of the most beautiful of all the braids. I have seen the pattern simulated in such unlikely materials as the stone of grave markers and the cloth appliqués of the Cameroons. The serpentine undulations of the strands are no doubt laden with symbolic implications in both China and Africa. But since these are not known to us, we are free to see our own significance in the pattern as it builds under our fingers. I like to think of it as a closely knit family, the core of dark at the center representing home and parents, the lighter strands, which leave and then return, as children whose lives are separate but still linked. You will see your own and different implications, if your mind enjoys this turn of thought.

The Chinese braid is a little more challenging to learn than some of the others in this book but it is well worth the effort. If you follow the directions step by step, with the yarns in your hand, and look carefully at the photographs and drawings, you should have no trouble mastering it. The important thing to keep in mind is that this is a weaving, and that after each step, the shed is changed.

Sixteen strands are needed, 4 dark, 8 medium, and 4 light. Or it may be made with 4 dark, 4 medium, and 8 light. For take-up, allow about one and a half times the finished length. After the strands are cut, tie them with an overhand knot into color pairs. The ends may be pinned down on a piece of building board with T-pins or placed under the clip of a clip board. The 2 pairs of darks go in the center. A medium pair, a light pair and a medium pair are placed on either side of the 2 dark pairs in the center.

Step 1. Weave the 4 dark yarns together. The first yarn right of center goes over the first one on the left of center and under the outside yarn of the left pair. The outside yarn of the right pair then weaves under and over to the left. This is the basic center weave and will be repeated whenever the dark yarns are in the center position.

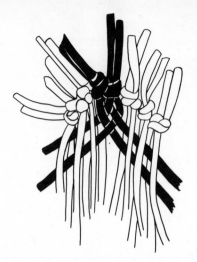

Step 2. *Make a shed* on both sides with the medium and light yarns by lifting one of each pair of yarns to the top. The *yarns closest to the center* are in the bottom shed. Lead the 2 dark wefts through this shed as though they were a single yarn. Now *change the shed* by bringing the top yarns down and lifting the lower yarns up.

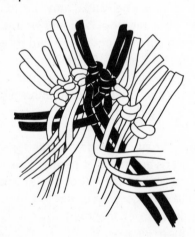

Step 3. The third step is a little like a club sandwich—with a set of 3 yarns (light and medium) in each layer. The dark yarns do not take part in this stacking up of layers. The third step is shown in a series of three drawings.

a. The top shed of 3 yarns on either side is laid aside to be out of the way. The right-hand group of 3 yarns is laid as a group to the left. This is the bottom layer of the sandwich. The lower shed from the left is crossed over them to the right. The lower groups have been crossed, left over right, and their ends point in opposite directions.

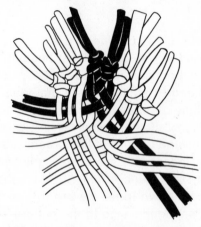

b. The top shed on the right is brought down and to the left, thus making all the yarns that previously were on the right point to the left.

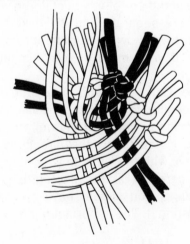

c. The 3 remaining yarns in the top shed at the left are brought down and to the right. This completes the crossing and stacking of groups. All 6 yarns which were at the right side are now at the left and those which were at the left are at the right.

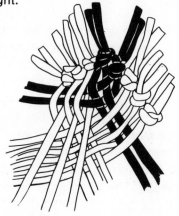

Step 5. Weave the center dark yarns just as you did in the beginning.

Step 6. *Change sheds* on both sides and lead the dark yarns to the outside just as you did in the second step. You are

Step 4. *Change sheds* at each side, bringing all the yarns that were in the lower shed to the top and the top ones to the bottom. Now bring the dark pair at the outside on the right into play again, carrying it in through the new shed back to the center where it started. The diagram shows the right-hand dark yarns returning to the center. The left-hand darks return, also.

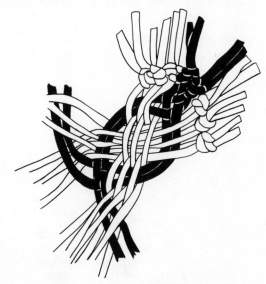

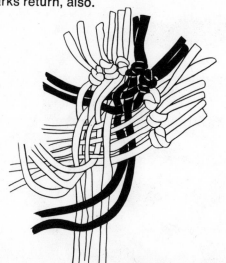

now starting the second unit. Continue with the various steps as described above. You are ready to repeat the third step as soon as you have again changed sheds.

Mel Kernahan's belt

Mel Kernahan braided a striking belt, using large roving which shows clearly how the units appear if they are done correctly. Black was used for the dark yarn. Hot pink and orange were used for the medium and light colors.

The appearance of the braid varies considerably with the materials used. Madeleine Wirth used jute, which is inexpensive and attractive. The black cords are dyed. They are used with natural and bleached jute. Sixteen strands were cut, each 3 yards long. These yielded 2 yards of braid including fringe. (Color Plate #74)

The Chinese braid makes an attractive trim for sweaters, skirts, jackets and coats. Many ethnic groups have made extensive use of handmade braids in their costumes. These provide inspiration for fashion designers today. We have seen peasant costumes from Greece which are so encrusted with beautiful braids that they seem almost able to stand alone. The Chinese braid lends itself to this type of costume embellishment.

Martha Bontems used knitting yarn to make a braid for a green sweater she had knitted. What would otherwise have

Madeleine Wirth's belt

been just another nice sweater became a highly original garment with the addition of the braid.

Widening the Chinese Braid to Any Width

One of the exciting things our group of craftsmen has been able to do was to discover how to make a wide Chinese braid. This should not be attempted until the narrow braid has been mastered. The principle of making a wide web instead of a narrow band is very simple. After the dark yarns have been led to the outside of their own group, they are woven with the adjoining dark yarns of the adjacent group.

To begin, all units are set up in pairs of yarns and pinned to a piece of building board. The first unit is carried to step two where the dark yarns are led to the outside. This is done in every unit across the entire width of the work. At this point, the two pairs of yarns which are in corresponding positions next to one another between each braid unit are woven together and "exchange places": the top right-hand dark thread crosses over the top left-hand dark thread and under the bottom left-hand thread. The bottom right-hand dark thread crosses under the top left-hand dark thread and over the bottom left-hand dark thread. When this has been done the dark yarns that came from the right side of the first unit have been woven into the dark yarns that came from the left of the second unit. This exchange continues across the entire width of the work. At either *edge* each dark pair will return to its own center as in a narrow braid.

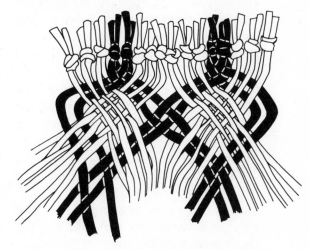

As the work progresses, all of the darks except the pair at either edge of the whole work will travel diagonally across the entire width. They need to be considerably longer than the other yarns.

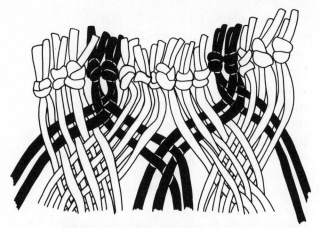

These traveling darks will assume an angle of about 45 degrees. This makes it easy to compute how long to cut them. For example, if you plan to fingerweave a small pillow 12 inches square, cut a piece of newspaper that size. Fold it from corner to corner diagonally and measure the length of the diagonal. It will be just short of 17 inches. We now know that to travel diagonally across a 12 x 12 inch pillow, the dark strands will move 17 inches. We now add a little more than one third—6 inches for easy measuring —for the take-up. But we must also add at least 4 more inches for ease of grasp at the completion of the braiding. This adds up to 27 inches but does not give us any allowance for a fringe at the beginning end of the braiding. So we add another 3 inches for that and cut our *dark* cords 30 inches long.

The medium cords and the light cords will be 12 inches plus one third (4 inches) plus 7 inches for handling and fringes, or a total of 23 inches. We cut 12 of these for each unit, usually 8 medium value and 4 light.

In the photograph we have left the units of the braid spaced out at some distance to show the movement of the strands. In actual practice they would lie snugly together. A unit braided from heavy rug yarn will measure about 1½ inches across. A unit braided from knitting yarn will measure about one inch across. To know exactly the width of a unit and therefore the number of units needed to produce a certain width, a sample should be made and measured. Not only do yarns vary a great deal but the tension each weaver produces also tends to vary.

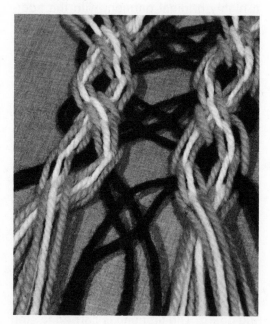

A PILLOW AND BAG IN CHINESE BRAID

Pat Holtz made our first wide Chinese braid. She used rug yarn, choosing a rich deep purple for the traveling darks, royal blue for the medium tone, and chartreuse for the lights. The pillow top was mounted on a dark blue pillow. We found it wise to make the pillow after the braid was completed because the exact size of the work is not easy to predict.

Pat's pillow is 12 x 15 inches. She braids quite snugly so she needed 11 units (instead of the 10 that would have been needed if each unit had been 1½ inches wide). There are 2 inches of fringe at each end. The yarns were cut according to the lengths given for the 12-inch square pillow. Each unit is the same length as in the square unit; there are just more units. The darks travel at the same diagonal slant regardless of the number of units.

To make a cylinder of Chinese braid, work around a piece of building board in which pins can be stuck. It should be the width of the finished work. Figure how long each single yarn needs to be, using the guide just given, and double that length, because these yarns will be middled and hung on a holding cord tied around the piece of building board. A larkshead knot is a good way to mount the cords.

After you have braided the first row around the board, you will know whether or not you need to add another unit to completely cover the board. Yarns tend to fluff out when they are hanging loosely so it may seem that you have enough ends, but after the braiding pulls them together this may not be the case.

Alcie Hendrickson used jute in black, natural and bleached tones to make a cylindrical tote bag. Black jute in the Egyptian braid makes the handle. A row of half hitches is made around the bag just under the larkshead knots before the braiding begins. The purpose of this is to give a firm beginning edge.

77

A SLEEVELESS JACKET
IN CHINESE BRAID

Orange, red, and white 4-ply acrylic knitting yarn was used for the sleeveless jacket that Martha Bontems braided for Jean Hudson, her instructor. Jean models the garment in the photograph. (Color Plate #78)

In this particular weight of yarn, one unit of the braid is an inch wide. Forty units were set up, unit by unit, and pinned to a large piece of building board over a paper pattern. The bottom of the jacket was the top starting place and a long fringe was left at the edge where the braiding began. There are no side seams. The entire circumference was braided up as far as the arm holes as a flat piece. The newspaper cut-out shows the general plan of the pattern.

The red yarn, being the darkest, needed to be cut longer than the other yarns because it moves across the work diagonally. If you follow the dark yarn upward from the bottom edge of the detailed photograph, you will see the path of each pair of dark yarns, first as the woven center of a unit, then as the woven joining of adjacent units.

To compute the length of the medium and light strands for a jacket, decide how long it is to be. Jean's jacket measures 27 inches from the center of the back of the neck to the bottom of the braiding. You may want yours either longer or shorter. Add a third of the length, or 9 inches, for take-up plus 4 inches on either end for working convenience. In the case of a 27-inch jacket, the medium and light strands are cut 44 inches long. This allows 9 inches for actual take-up and 4 inches on each end for finishing and handling.

To figure how long the dark strands need to be, cut a square piece of paper using the length of the jacket at center back as a measurement. Fold this paper diagonally from corner to corner and measure the length of this "bias fold" of

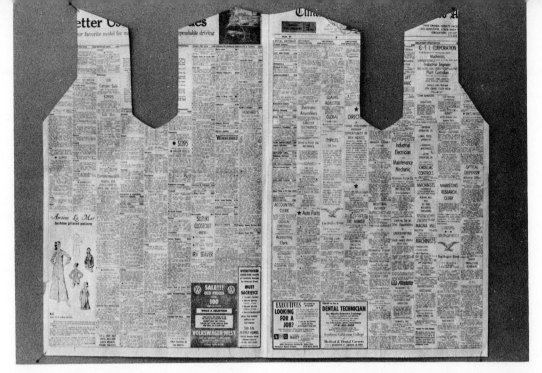

paper. Add a third to this length for take-up, and again 4 inches at either end for fringe and handling. If the square of paper is 27 inches on each side, the diagonal will be approximately 38 inches. Add to this for take-up and ends to arrive at 44 inches for the length of the dark yarns. Those which will eventually arrive under the arm holes do not need to be this long but it is better to waste a few ends than to risk running short.

When the body of the jacket had been braided as far as the arm holes, four units were dropped on each side. Later the ends were finished off with a row of double half hitches, using one of the yarns as a cord over which to knot. The half hitches gave a firm edge. The first step of the Damascus edge (see the chapter on finishing techniques) was used to turn the ends to the back where they were snipped off. A band of hand-sewn lace keeps the ends in place.

The remaining units continued toward the shoulder except at the neck line where the braiding stopped according to the edge of the pattern. The braiding ceased, one unit at a time, following the somewhat diagonal line of the shoulders. A row of double half hitches firmed up each shoulder edge where the braiding stopped. The ridges made by the hitching were turned to the wrong side of the garment and these were sewed together with a needle and some of the yarn, making a simple seam.

A length of Kru Coast braid (see the chapter on square and round braids) finishes the edge of the neck and makes the ties in the front.

8 Mexican Double Weaving

From ancient Peru and from contemporary Mexico comes a beautiful double cloth. It is braided with two separate sets of strands, usually a light set and a dark set for contrast. At intervals, the color which is being worked on the back or "wrong" side of the fabric is brought to the top side, thread between thread of the upper layer. This may sound complicated, but the actual technique is very easy. In calling the work Mexican double weaving, instead of giving it a Peruvian description, we are again following the lead of Mary Meigs Atwater, whose book, *Byways in Handweaving,* has for many years been a classic of rare weaving techniques.

The best way to learn Mexican double weaving is to begin with a sample—a relatively flat belt. Later, you will learn how to make a cylindrical bag or pillow. Light and dark yarns are needed. Cut 6 lengths about 2 yards long from each color value. These will be doubled—or middled—and mounted at the center of a holding cord with a larkshead knot. Refer back to page 17 if you have forgotten how to mount cords with a larkshead knot. Mount cords

alternately on the holding cord, first a dark pair, then a light pair. The holding cord may be pinned at both ends to a piece of building board or placed under the clip of a clipboard to hold all the yarns in place. Since each cord was middled, there are now 12 ends of light and 12 ends of dark, set in alternate pairs.

Step 1. Begin weaving with the light strands. Because the yarns are in pairs, there is automatically an even number of

MEXICAN DOUBLE WEAVING

light strands. Even numbers are necessary. Find the middle space of the light group. Cross the first yarn at the right of the middle space over the first yarn at the left of the middle space.

Step 3. Bring the fourth cord in from the left and pass it over and under those that have come from the right.

Step 2. Pick up the first uninvolved cord on the right and bring it under the cord that came from the left. Three cords are now involved.

Step 4. Continue the weaving, picking up a strand from one side, then the other, and incorporating it into the work until all strands have been involved and a point has been woven.

Step 5. Lift the light point up out of the way and weave the dark yarns into a similar point.

Step 6. Lock the dark and light points together by bringing the light cords down over the dark ones, and then bringing the dark yarns to the surface, one between each light cord. This forms a shed.

Step 7. Weave the outside dark cord on the right edge to the center through the other dark cords, as though you were doing the Peruvian flat braid.

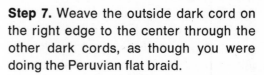

Step 8. Weave each dark cord in turn in toward the center. When the sixth cord has been woven, there will be no remaining cords for it to weave through, so simply turn it toward the center of the braid.

Step 9. Weave the dark cords on the left side of the unit in the same way that those on the right have been braided. There is now a little dark triangle on each side of the braid.

Step 10. Flip the dark woven triangles out of the way and weave the light yarns on each side into triangles similar to the dark ones.

Step 11. Bring the dark woven triangle on the right down over the light one and change sheds. This is done on both sides.

Step 12. Now you will weave the first complete diamond shape in the light cords. To begin, cross the top light cord on the right of center over the top light cord on the left.

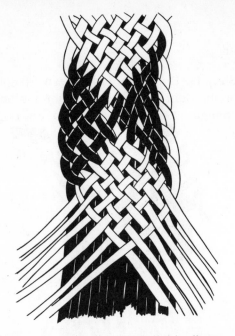

Step 13. Complete the light diamond shape by involving a cord alternately from one side, then the other, just as the beginning point was formed. After the diamond has been woven, 6 cords protrude from it to the right and 6 to the left.

Step 14. The braid is now turned completely over and a dark diamond shape is woven in the same way as the light one on the other side. The sheds are then changed. This step is not illustrated because the diamond is woven just as in Step 13.

Have you guessed the next step? The braid is turned over, a light diamond shape is woven as in Step 1, and the dark cords are once again brought to the surface, one between each light yarn.

The weaving continues for its entire length, repeating locked diamonds bounded by triangular shapes.

A BELT IN MEXICAN DOUBLE WEAVING

Doris Fox used heavy rug yarns, blue and white, to make a long belt in Mexican double weaving. (Color Plate #9)

The belt has fringe at both ends so the strands were not middled at the beginning. Twelve white yarns and 12 blue yarns were cut, each 132 inches long. This length is one and a half times the finished length of 72 inches, plus 12 inches at each end for fringe.

The dimensional quality in Doris' belt was achieved by lifting the light triangles after they were braided, turning them in toward one another at the center and securing the edges together, in this case with cherry red yarn.

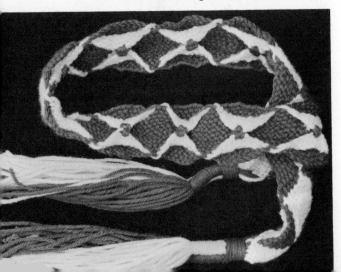

MEXICAN DOUBLE WEAVING

The red yarn was also introduced in the wrapping at the ends of the belt.

A HERALDIC BANNER IN MEXICAN DOUBLE WEAVING

Starting with the idea that a double woven wall hanging might be made with just one large diamond shape in the center, Pat Holtz selected paprika red and moss green rug yarn for her project.

The red yarns were braided together in small 3-strand braids down to the place the big diamond would begin. A diamond shape out of hardboard was used as a gauge over which to work. The threads were knotted in groups with overhand knots to mark the edge of the diamond. The hanging was flipped over and the green yarns were treated in the same way. While Pat was weaving the red yarns, the board was immediately beneath them, the green yarns below the board. When she turned the work over to weave the green yarns, the board remained between the layers of yarn, and she decided to leave the hardboard inside the diamond permanently to give it body and weight. It is held in place by the overhand knots which complete the 4 sides of the diamond.

One side of the hanging is a red diamond with a green background. The other side is the reverse. It can be viewed from either side or both. There is a heraldic quality about this simple bold statement. It makes one think of cathedrals or of knights carrying banners into jousts.

Even though this hanging is quite large (15 x 35 inches), it is a single unit of Mexican double weaving. We will now take up the method of weaving 2 or more units together. (*See page 86*)

85

A LEARNING SAMPLE
THAT BECAME A WALL HANGING

Abigail Donnelly made her learning sample of the double Mexican weave on a twig of weathered wood. The sample was very attractive and it seemed worthwhile to add more braiding to utilize the width of the stick, so Abigail hung additional yarns onto the stick on either side of the learning sample. These yarns were made into Kru Coast braids (p. 98) and Peruvian flat braids (page 22). All of the yarns were brought together at the bottom of the hanging. (Color Plate #12)

Weaving Two or More Units Together in a Flat Mexican Weave

A flat braid may be made as wide as one wishes in Mexican double weaving. A little experimenting with the yarn material you plan to use will determine how many units of a certain number of cords per unit are needed to make the desired width. In the following diagrams, you will see 2 units, in each of which there are 6 light pairs of yarns and 6 dark pairs. To make the set-up, a light pair and a dark pair alternate in the braiding clamp or on a piece of building board. We have separated the units slightly so each group shows as a unit; in actual practice

the groups would be set closer together. In the sample, you may decide to add several additional units.

The directions for the Mexican double weave, which uses a single unit, should be read before attempting to make the wider one. The only different thing about the wider braid is the method of joining units by weaving them together.

Step 1. After setting up 2 units with dark and light pairs alternating (6 pairs of each in both units) the light yarns in each unit are woven to a point and flipped up out of the way while the dark ones are woven into 2 similar points.

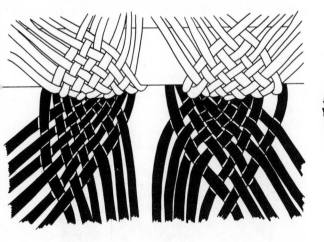

Step 2. The light points are brought down over the dark ones and lie on top of them. The sheds are changed. The 6 light yarns from the right hand unit which project toward the left are woven through the 6 light yarns which project toward them from the left-hand unit. This forms a diamond shape. *The two units are now united.*

Step 3. The 6 darks from the right-hand side are woven through the 6 darks from the adjacent left-hand side. This diamond shape rests on top of the light one woven in the second step.

Step 4. The yarns at the side of the diamonds are worked as though this were a single unit of Mexican double weaving. To weave the right-hand edge, the 6 dark yarns are flipped up out of the way and the light yarns are woven, one at a time, toward the center.

Step 5. The dark yarns, which were laid aside while the light ones at the edge were being woven, are taken in hand and woven into a triangle. This triangle lies on top of the light one, which was woven in step 4. The sheds are then changed.

Step 6. The weaving goes forward to form a diamond shape in each unit of the braid just as though a single unit were being woven. Light diamonds lie on top of dark diamonds, the shed is changed in each unit, and you are ready to continue with a diamond shape that uses 6 yarns from each of the adjacent units and weaves the units together.

PURSES, BAGS AND PILLOWS IN DOUBLE WEAVE

The only new thing to learn about the double weave before starting a cylindrical object is that you must set up the cords in a circle. Usually this is a length of yarn or string tied around a piece of building board cut to the desired width. Single strands are mounted with an overhand knot—dark and light alternating—if you wish a fringe at both ends. For a bag or purse, the strands are usually cut twice the required length, middled, and tied on the holding cord with larkshead knots. The required length should always be at least one and a half times the finished length, plus at least 4 inches, to hold to at the end of the braiding. This extra yarn for working convenience may be used as fringe at the bottom or knotted and cut off. (See the chapter on finishing techniques.)

Eight light ends and 8 dark ends make a good working unit. When 4 middled strands of light and 4 of dark have been mounted alternately on the holding cord,

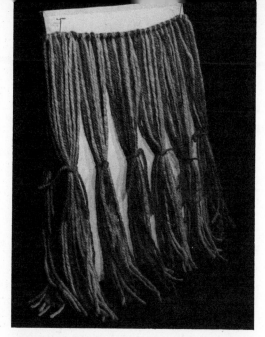

Braid the light cords in each unit into similar points, working all the way around the board. After each group of 8 strands is braided to a point, 4 cords will extend obliquely to the right, 4 to the left.

Raise the light woven yarns out of the way above the holding cord and repeat the process of braiding a point in each unit of dark yarn. Bring the light points

totalling 8 ends of light and 8 of dark, tie them loosely in bundles of 16 alternating colors with an extra length of string to keep them in sets. If the circle seems to be filled with yarn and the final set is not complete, push the yarns together to make room for a complete unit.

After the strands have been mounted, untie the restraining cord around any one unit and lift the light cords up in the hand to begin to braid that unit into a point, just as described in the learning sample.

down over the dark points. Bring the dark yarns to the surface, thread between thread, just as you did in the learning sample when changing sheds.

A row of dark complete diamond

B. J. Koch's bag

shapes (rather than points) is now woven all around the board. These are raised out of the way while a similar circle of light diamonds are woven. Once again the matching woven areas are placed, one above the other, and the sheds are changed.

Interesting textures add greatly to the beauty of bags made in double weave. B. J. Koch used an unexpected combination—white seine cord with creamy knitting yarn—for a beautifully crafted bag lined in canvas to give it body and strength. The understated color contrast

is as delightful as the texture. The bag measures 12 inches across and is 10 inches deep.

Twenty-four units were required to make this dimension. There are 8 ends of seine cord and 8 ends of yarn in each unit. After the beginning row of points, 9 complete diamonds were woven before ending the bag with overhand knots. The beautiful workmanship is a further attraction of this bag.

The gusset strap, which forms the handle, is braided from the same materials as the bag and is made like the learning sample for double braiding.

Celia Wagner used rows of overhand knots to give added texture to her purse. Celia's bag also is lined with canvas. Overhand knots are also used to join the two sides at the bottom of the bag.

Anne Daniels wove her magenta and chartreuse bag in a cylinder and gathered the bottom together with a tassel. Anne experimented with the arrangement of the diamond shapes and did not

Eunice Ewing's pillow

switch colors from back to front regularly. Two round braided cords act as drawstrings to close the bag at the top.

Eunice Ewing wove her pillow in the same way that the bags were woven—as a cylinder—but with both ends sewed shut. The pillow is more loosely braided than the bags, allowing the lining to show slightly. (Color Plate #1)

Right—Celia Wagner's bag
Below—Anne Daniel's bag

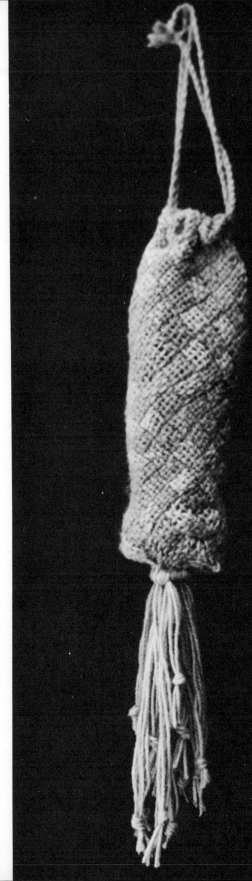

JEAN HUDSON'S WALL HANGING

Jean Hudson set out to see how freely double fingerweaving might be done. Her first innovation was to set up her yarns with the light values in three sections rather than in alternating light and dark pairs. Her dark yarns are reds, blue, magenta, and purple, all about the same value. The light yarns are a mixture of pink, gold, peach, and yellow green. There is a great variety of size and texture. Included are two knitting yarns used together as though they were a single strand. Other yarns are fatter.

Jean braided the dark cords down, group by group, forming points. The three groups of light cord were braided together on the back with the flat Peruvian weave. At any time in the progress of a Peruvian flat braid, the edge slopes from one side to the other. This enabled Jean to bring the light cords to the forward side of the weaving, which was also at an angle, whenever she thought it needed a flash of light color.

The hanging, which is 18 inches wide, grew to a length of 56 inches without any preconceived plan. It may be seen from either or both sides. When it was finished, the small pockets formed by the emergence and disappearance of the light yarns on the surface seemed just the place for a small child to hide small treasures—a polished pebble, a shell, a bright bit of glass, so Jean's hanging be-

MEXICAN DOUBLE WEAVING

came "A Home for Small Treasures."

Jean ended her hanging with four dark points in front of three light points. Large overhand knots at the bottom secure and group the fringe.

This way of working should not be too difficult for anyone who has been able to follow the directions for Doris Fox's belt. It simply adapts that technique to working free interchanges between the light and dark threads.

9 Square and Round Braids

Square and round braids have been used for practical purposes throughout history—as carrying ropes, humble little donkey muzzles, fringes, handles, belts, and many more. Some of these woven braids are formed with as few as four strands, but by using several strands as one, an enormous number may be involved. Often a braid is worked around a thick core at the center to give it body and to prevent stretching. A braid formed over a core is called a coxcomb. Today weavers may use these braids as a delightful way to end a weaving, but to relegate them to the category of an adjunct to flat weaving is to fail to explore their potential.

Four-Strand Round Indian Braid

The 4-strand round braid is usually used in fringe but even as few as 4 strands may become a coxcomb.

To learn the braid, use 2 strands each of 2 colors—one light and one dark. Pin them in pairs to a piece of building board. Take the light strands in the left hand, the dark ones in the right.

Step 1. Pick up the outside dark strand, move it behind the other dark strand and behind one of the light strands. Bring it up to the top side between the light strands and place it back in the right-hand group. It will then be the strand in the right-hand group that is nearest the center.

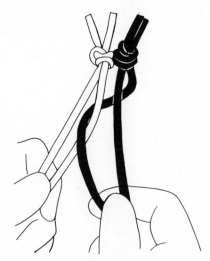

Step 2. Make the same cycle with the outside light strand, bringing it behind

the second light strand, allowing it to surface between the darks before returning to its fellow on the left.

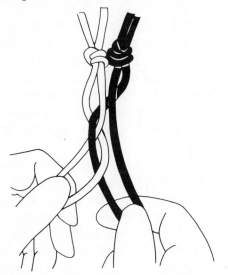

Step 3. Continue the braid with the 2 cycles described. Bringing a dark outside cord up between the 2 light cords repeats step 1.

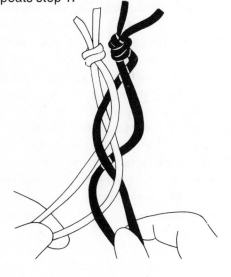

This simple braid is rapidly done as soon as the hand motions are mastered. Hold the strands taut as you work to make the pattern distinct and the tension even.

If the lights and the darks are arranged differently, that is with 1 dark and 1 light in each hand, a different pattern results.

Kristin Levin used this arrangement in the 4-strand round Indian braid to finish the long fringe on her belt of Peruvian flat braid.

Jo Dendel used this braid to finish his afghan. The yarn colors make a delightful pattern and give the afghan a finished look. Since the number of yarns across the bottom of his afghan did not divide evenly by 4, a pair of ends were worked as a single cord in the braid where necessary. A detail of the afghan edge is pictured in the chapter on finishing techniques.

If a core is used, the motions are not changed. When the outside dark strand is moved behind the other dark strand and one of the light strands, it is also moved behind the core. In a similar manner the light outside strand is brought behind the second light strand, the core, and one of the dark strands before it surfaces and returns to its own side.

Four strands will not cover a very large core. A core the thickness of ordinary coat-hanger wire is about the limit. To cover larger cores it is better to use the 6-strand round braid or the Egyptian braid.

The Six-Strand Round Braid

The 6-strand round braid is beautiful and useful. It covers a core much more adequately than the 4-strand round braid. Working around a core is easier if the core is stretched taut and raised a little above the working surface. An excellent arrangement can be made by fastening a C-clamp to the edge of a piece of building board to be used as an anchor for the core.

An overhand knot is tied in one end of the core and pinned down on the board at a place where it is convenient to begin work. The core is led from this spot to the clamp at the edge of the board and wrapped around it an inch or so above the surface. The loose far end of the core is then pinned down to the board at the side of the clamp. Additional length of the core strand can be fed out from the clamp as needed when the braid progresses.

The take-up of the braid—and consequently how much yarn or cord you will need—will vary with the size of the core. Using a rope slightly larger than a clothesline, strands which were cut a yard long yielded 18 inches of braid. One can not braid to the very ends of the strands because several inches of ends are needed for grasping.

With the core cord stretched tightly, you are ready to make the beginning arrangement of the braiding strands. With an overhand knot, tie 2 dark strands and 1 light one together and place them at the immediate left of the core, with the light piece closest to the core. Similarly, place 2 light strands and 1 dark one at the right of the core with the dark one next to the core. Lead the light strand at the left to the right, crossing the core. Cross the right hand one to the left over the core and over the light one which just crossed the core. All the light cords are now on the right and all the dark ones on the left. This is the starting position.

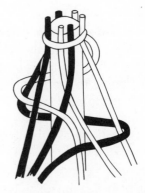

Step 1. Pick up the outside right strand and lead it to the left behind the core and *all* of the strands, both light and dark. Weave it back to the right by going over, under, over the dark strands at the left of the core.

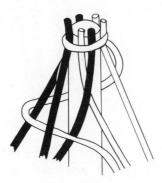

The weaving strand rejoins the strands on the right and takes its place as the closest strand to the core.

Step 2. Pick up the outside left—or dark —strand. Lead it behind all of the strands and the core. Weave it back to the left by weaving over, under, over.

Simply repeat these two steps for the length of the braid. Wrapping both ends for a short distance keeps it from coming undone.

Even though this is a round braid it is much easier to learn if you think of it as a flat braid with a right and a left side. It helps to stretch the 3 cords on either side out tautly so there is no confusion about their order. It is always a top, outside strand which moves.

97

If you have to leave the work and come back to it, it helps to know that the cord that should be worked is always the top, outside cord which *comes out from under* a cord going to the other side. The right-hand outside cord moves to the left under all the cords and weaves back to the right. The left-hand cord moves to the right under all the cords and weaves back to the left.

The cord makes an excellent drawstring for bags.

The Eight-Strand Kru Coast Braid

The Kru tribesmen, the only group in Liberia who like to go to sea, are the people who taught me this braid. For reasons they had either forgotten or failed to tell me, they called it "Holding Back the Stream." It was not until I later read Clifford W. Ashley's *Book of Knots* that I learned that this braid actually is used as a gasket on steam pipes on ships.

In Nigeria I found the same braid used to cinch loads of wood on little donkeys, and also as lead ropes and muzzles for donkeys. In North Africa, especially in Morocco, it is used to make belts.

Three feet of cord will yield about 2 feet of braid. It is more easily learned and the pattern shows more clearly if 2 colors are used. Jute and seine cord are a subtle combination. Rug yarn is another good material.

Cut 8 strands the desired length, 4 of each color. Secure the ends in a clip-

board. Place the light-colored yarns on the left.

Step 1. Pick up an outside light cord on the left and pass it to the right behind the other light cords and behind 2 of the dark ones. Bring it to the top surface, lay it to the left over the 2 dark yarns nearest the center, and return it to its fellow light yarns, this time on the *inside* of the group.

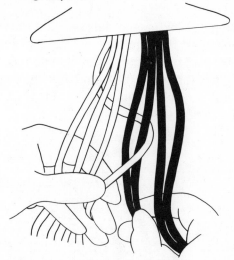

Hold the light cords firmly taut in the left hand. As you work with each cord pull it free from the group to avoid tangles.

Step 2. Pick up the dark cord on the outside right, pass it to the left behind the other dark cords and two of the light cords. Return it to its fellow dark cords, allowing it to come to rest on the inside of the group.

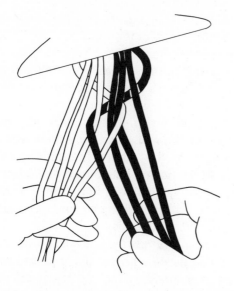

groups. If working on a clipboard and you are interrupted, take each group around to the back of the board and tie them together. This will keep the braid from rolling and spoiling the pattern sequence.

Continue these steps, using the outside cord each time and returning it to the inside position in its own color group. Keep the yarns taut at all times and when it is necessary to pause, tie them in

99

In Morocco, belts are made of two rows of the braid. To do this, cut the cords twice as long as the usual length cut for a single-strand belt. Since there is a one-third take-up in this braid, a single-braid belt 6 feet long will require strands 8 feet long; a double 16 feet.

Begin braiding in the center of the length. Double the first 6 inches of the braid back on itself and tie together with a few buttonhole loops (or half hitches).

Continue braiding each group of 8 strands, joining them at intervals as you wish. When the belt is worn, the loop in the center can be used to secure it by dropping the other end of the belt through the loop. The free end may be weighted with beads or pompoms. Eunice Ewing's belt is made with 2 rows of braid and a center loop.

To join the braids at intervals, take 4 strands from one and work them with 4 strands of the other. The photograph shows the beginning motions of the braid in which the outside strand from one side moves between the pair on the other side. (*See top, opposite*)

Working with white and rust cords, the light cords were held in the left hand and the dark ones in the right just as described in the directions above. After making 8 inches of braid, the work was bent into a loop, bringing the beginning down to the working area. This loop was held together with tight half hitches. (See the chapter on finishing techniques to learn how to do half hitches.) After the half hitching was done, 16 ends protruded. These were regrouped into sets

Eunice Ewing's belt

of 8 before the work continued in 2 parallel square braids.

Cords may be regrouped, braided for equal distances, and then grouped in a different way whenever one wishes. One possibility for rearrangement is to work the 8 light cords together and the 8 dark ones together for a parallel distance, after which 4 from each set make the new arrangement.

Colors are usually arranged with light on one side and dark on the other for ease of learning, but after one has learned the braid, it is interesting to play with the color arrangement. Recently I saw a very old American Indian braid of horsehair, which was made like a Kru Coast square braid except that many strands were used as one for each of the 8 cords and the colors alternated light, dark, light, dark, throughout the 8 strands instead of being grouped into lights and darks.

The square Kru Coast braid combines nicely with wrapped areas, the round and the square areas enhancing one another. The section of a bell pull by Jo Dendel is in orange, magenta, and red yarns. It hangs against a mahogany wall.

Flat-Sided Variation of the Kru Coast Braid

Although it is neither round nor flat we include this braid here because it is very like the square Kru Coast braid. The setup is the same—4 light cords on the left, 4 dark ones on the right.

Pick up the first light cord, pass it behind the other three light cords and bring it up to the surface after passing it under only 1 of the dark cords. (In the square braid, the light cord surfaced after passing under 2 of the dark cords.) Place it back in the left hand with the other light cords. It will be an inside cord.

Now pick up the outside dark cord, pass it under its fellows and under one of the lights, after which it returns to its own kind in the center area.

Continue working, first from the left, then from the right. The only difficulty you are likely to encounter is starting again after you have stopped. If possible, stop with all the light strands on the left and all the dark ones on the right. Each group may be brought to the back of a clipboard and tied in a bow knot.

If you get confused at any place during the braiding, take the work back to a place where 4 cords issue from each side, one above the other.

A DOOR WREATH
IN KRU COAST AND ROUND BRAIDS

Cindy Hickok started her door wreath with an 8-inch metal hoop, a 4-inch metal hoop, some lengths of copper wire for the smaller circles, and 5 handmade bells from Uganda. The wreath may be used instead of a doorbell or it may be hung in the patio as wind chimes.

The circumference of the big hoop is approximately 27 inches. A third of that, 9 inches, was added for take-up, and 4 inches for ease of handling at the end, making each strand 40 inches long. Cindy used rug yarn in orange and gold-green, 4 strands of each. The Kru Coast braid was worked around the metal hoop, using the metal like a core. The beginning and the ending of the braid were covered with wrapping at the place they met. Four additional circles were attached at this point.

Each bell has 2 holes in the top. Yarns were middled and pulled through these holes with a needle to make the part of the wreath which hangs down from the metal hoop. Three of these braided hangings are in 4-strand round Indian braids and 2 are in the Kru Coast square braid.

Christmas wreaths may be braided in a similar way with sleigh bells hanging from the wreath.

The Egyptian Braid
The Egyptian braid has an ancient history going back to the time of Rameses

and probably earlier. It is enormously useful, and may be made either with or without a core. Since a core prevents stretching, the braid is usually made as a coxcomb. It may be made with many strands but for an easy learning project, we use 12 strands—4 dark, 8 light—plus the core. Cut the braiding strands twice the length desired in the finished braid.

Tie an overhand knot in the core and pin it in the center of the working area. Seine cord or clothesline make a good core. Arrange the braiding cords on both sides of the core. Tie 2 of the darks together and pin them at the immediate right of the core. Tie the 2 remaining dark strands together, pin them at the immediate left of the core, opposite the first pair. Having a pair of dark cords on either side of the core makes it easier to keep the sequence in order. Tie and pin a pair of light strands on either side of the core next to the darks. Next, pin another light pair on each side.

The basic movement in the Egyptian braid is crossing the core from one side, then from the other side, alternately, with a pair of strands, one strand of which goes on top of the core and one beneath.

Step 1. Take the right-hand dark pair to the left across the core with one strand on top of the core and one beneath it. These dark strands come to rest next to the core on the left-hand side.

Step 2. Bring the dark pair that was pinned at the left of the core across it to the right. It will lie next to the core on the right side. The pairs of cords have now changed sides.

Step 3. The light pair of cords closest to the center on the right is brought across the core, one strand on top and one beneath. This pair comes to rest on the left side of the core and closest to it.

Step 5. The outside right pair of light cords is brought across the core to the left.

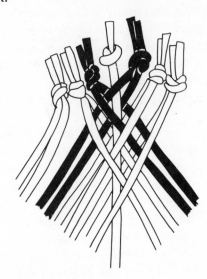

Step 4. The corresponding light pair on the left is brought across the core to the right in the same way.

Step 6. The left outside pair is brought across the core to the right.

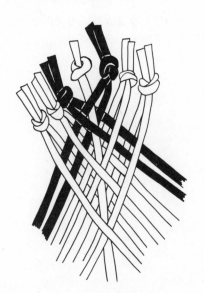

All of the cords have now been brought across the core and are on the side opposite to the one from which they were originally pinned.

We are now ready to begin the actual braiding, which continues to bring the cords in pairs, first from one side, then from the other, across the core. There is a new motion added now as the braiding begins, which did not take place in the steps described above. Each pair is given a twist, forming an "X" before it crosses the core.

Step 7. The dark pair on the right is given a twist, which is comparable to changing sheds because it brings the lower cord to the top. The crossed right pair is held in the right hand and brought to the left across the other cords on the right of the core, enclosing them.

Step 8. The dark pair, which was twisted and brought toward the core in Step 7, continues across the core and comes to rest on the left side, closest to the core.

Step 9. The dark pair on the left-hand side is now twisted and brought to the right across the strands at the left of the core and across the core.

Step 10. Continue the twisting and crossing. When all the pairs have been twisted and brought across the core, one cycle of the braid has been completed. This continues for the length of the braid.

It is quite possible and often desirable to make the Egyptian braid entirely of one color. This is a little more difficult because one must keep in mind the order of the moves without guidance from color differences. Leading the cords after each crossing to the edge of a board and pinning them there is a help in keeping order.

This fellow has fiery orange hair.

A number of the purse handles in this book are made of Egyptian braid. To be sure that the core does not slip within the finished braid, an overhand knot may be tied at each end and covered by a wrapping of yarns.

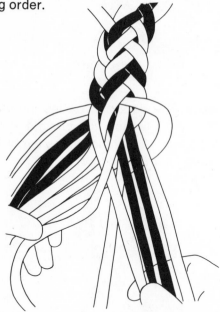

Bici Linklater played with bright yarns and a length of rope to make a gay figure. The flare at the bottom of the legs is formed by braiding over the ends of the rope, which has been doubled back on itself to get it out of sight. The colors are orange, yellow-green and yellow.

106

A HANGING PLANTER USING THE EGYPTIAN BRAID

Mary Margaret Haeckel combined 6 embroidery hoops, assorted beads and light and dark jute cords to make a decorative hanging device for a brass planter.

The first step was to wrap the hoops so they could be inserted any place in the work where they were needed, either to hold the weight of the plant or to spread the braids apart. Since this project was not preplanned, areas of wrapping were used where it was necessary to add to the length of the cords. This is a device all braiders find useful. (See the chapter on finishing techniques.)

A hook of Egyptian braid makes the hanger for the hoops at the top. Repeating this pattern beneath the planter gives unity to the design. Keeping the patterned braids at some distance from the growing plant avoids competition between the design of the leaves and the strong pattern of light and dark zigzags in the braid.

The plain dark braids that support the brass bowl divide to receive the wrapped hoops, incorporating them organically into the work.

107

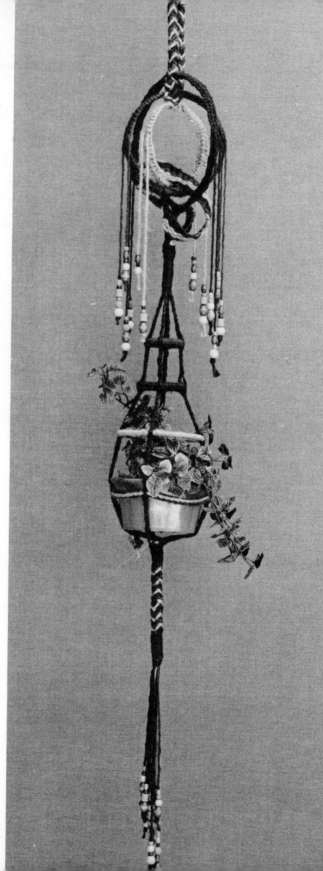

HORSE GEAR USING THE EGYPTIAN BRAID

Several girls in Celia Wagner's workshop for young people have made gear for their horses using the Egyptian braid. Lead ropes and halters in jute have been great fun for them to make and use.

Kathy Lilenthal, age 14, braided a special working bridle for her horse, Bonnie. It is called a "Split Ear Head Stall." It goes over only one of the horse's ears. Kathy cut seine cord and horse hair twice the length needed and followed the design used for this sort of lightweight working bridle. Monkey-fist

knots with a bead inside are used as buttons so the snaffle bit can be changed if desired.

Cindy Korman used three colors of heavy rug yarn over a strong rope core to make a lead line for her horse.

Maggie Dodd's lead line is made out of seine cord and natural and dyed dark jute. The joining of the ends of the braiding is covered with wrapping. The fibers are teased out into a bushy tassel at the ends.

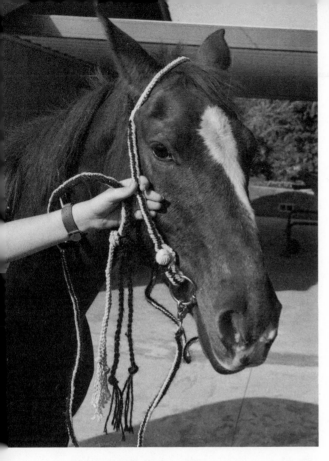

Making some of the gear which is used in working with one's horse adds depth and intimacy to the relationship between animal and owner.

109

10 Widening, Narrowing, and Shaping

Much potential use of fingerweaving is cancelled out if it is kept the same width along its entire course. Knowing how to drop strands, how to add strands, how to shape a piece of work to a given pattern, and how to add variety with changes of tension opens up endless new possibilities. In the chapter on the Peruvian flat braid you can see how Mary Jean Fowler added interest and texture to her work by varying the tension.

Usually a *pair* of strands is added or subtracted to a fingerweaving project in order to avoid interrupting the under-and-over sequence of the work. However, in the Peruvian flat braid, *single* strands may be added or dropped as one wishes. This is because the weft always comes from the same side and an extra strand or one less on the far edge makes no difference.

To drop a strand out of a Peruvian braid, start it through the shed alongside the strand that would normally be the next weft. This *pair* of wefts starts through the shed together but somewhere in the central area of the work, the one to be dropped is pulled to the

back and later snipped off. The remaining weft continues to the edge without the dropped strand.

Jean Hudson fingerwove a tie for her husband in colors which shaded from maroon through red to orange, gold, and yellow. She followed a commercial tie pattern, starting at the bottom on the widest end and dropping yarns as described above to make a smoothly sloping shape. In the photograph, you can see the dropped cords on the back before they were snipped off. (Color Plate #10)

At the bottom of the tie, the ends are tied in color groups by wrapping 1 yarn around 2 others with an overhand knot.

Widening a Peruvian flat braid by one strand is accomplished by introducing a new strand from the back and weaving it along with the working weft to the left edge. Both strands then hang down in turn and become warps on the left and the work has been widened by 1 strand.

The shed is changed as usual and the work progresses.

Widening any Fingerweaving by Adding a Pair of Strands

An added cord may be middled and dropped at the midpoint of its length over a weft in the preceding row. A shed

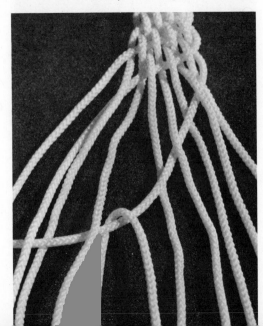

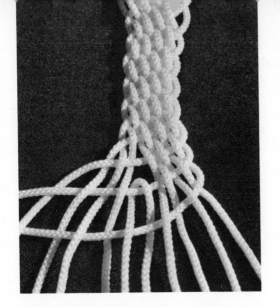

is made through all the warps including the two ends which have been added.

This is an inconspicuous way to add to the width of any of the over-one, under-one flat sennits. Doris Fox used this method to add strands in both of her braided chairs and you will see other examples of this device by studying the photographs throughout the book.

MAKING A DECORATIVE COLLAR OUT OF ADDED STRANDS

In edge-to-center braiding and in center-to-edge braiding, the middled added strand may be hung over the center crossing of strands to form a decorative pattern.

This method of adding strands is most often used when there are repeated additions at regular intervals.

Shaping a Braided Collar to a Pattern

Jean Hudson explored the possibility of braiding to an exact shape by working over a commercial pattern for a collar. The materials are rattail cord, chenille, several weights of knitting yarns and novelty yarns. This assortment gives variety of texture. About half of the cords are the round rattail, which is smooth and makes a good contrast for the textured cords. The colors are rusts and greens with some gold tones. (Color Plate #5)

To begin, Jean cut 84 cords, each 3 yards long. These were grouped in sets of 4 yarns. One yarn of each group was tied in an overhand knot around the

the cords one below the other to find a natural progression. These 21 lovely braids dangle between the right and left halves of the collar like jeweled chains. When the lengths had been established, each braid was tied with an overhand knot.

Braiding the Sides of the Collar

The paper pattern was pinned to a piece of building board and the first row of overhand knots where the round braiding began was pinned to the front edge of the left half of the pattern.

All of the cords in the 4-strand round braids were spread out flat to make the warps for the Peruvian flat braid. The first weft starts from the inside of the collar and nestles against the overhand knots which finish the round braids.

The photograph shows the beginning rows of Peruvian flat braiding.

other 3 in the set a yard from the beginning ends. This is preparatory to making the 4-strand round braids in the center front of the collar.

Making the Round Cords

The 4-strand round braiding was begun in the long end of each group immediately below the overhand knot. See the directions for this round braid in the chapter on square and round braids. The shortest braid in the group which connects the halves of the collar is less than an inch long. The longest braid at the bottom of the swag of braids is 22 inches long. Those in between the shortest and the longest progress gradually in length. The lengths were worked out by draping

Adding Strands to the Outside Edge

In order to widen the outside edge of the collar when necessary to conform to the pattern, Jean middled an extra cord and wove it from the center area to the outside edge, thus adding 2 strands.

Jean also found that she had to drop a few strands near the inside edge of the collar in order to rapidly change the contour of the collar. By adding cords at the outside and dropping some on the inside, the collar was made to fit the pattern.

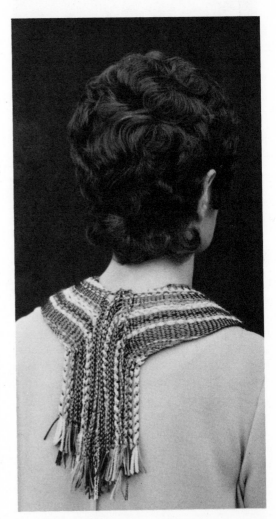

The next weft to come from the inside edge of the collar passes through all the warps including the 2 that have been added and which hang at the outside edge.

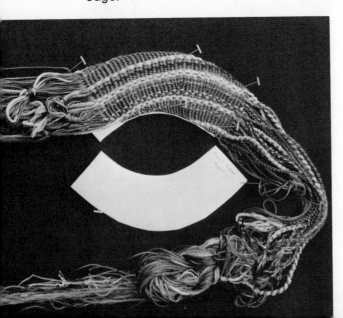

Weaving the Second Half of the Collar

To begin the second half of the collar, the overhand knots which had been tied at the ends of the round braids were brought to the front edge of the right-hand half of the collar pattern and pinned in place. The second half was then woven just like the first half except that the Peruvian flat braid, in order to move from the inside edge of the collar to the outside edge, had to be braided from left to right.

Braiding the Back Ends of the Collar

When the second half of the collar had been woven, Jean braided the ends into 4-strand round braids like the ones which hang in the front. The braid on either side of the center back was braided long enough to tie. These hold the collar together. The other ends were braided to lengths that form a point at the center back. Overhand knots finish the ends of the braids.

11 Finishing Techniques

Wrapping

Wrapping is a good way to secure ends at the completion of a fingerweaving. It is also useful—and very often highly original—to intersperse wrapping with braiding in the body of a work. Many of the projects in this book have wrapped areas which you will note as you page through the photographs.

The secret of a well-wrapped cord is to have both the starting ends and the finishing ends well buried.

A loop, preferably of a different color, is placed under the wrapping cord specifically to pull the final end back under what has been wrapped.

To begin, place the loop lengthwise alongside the cords to be wrapped. Leaving a generous length at the end of the wrapping cord, and keeping the end pointed toward the loop, wind the wrapping cord around the whole arrangement, over and over, toward the loop and covering completely the beginning end as you go. A desirable distance to bury the beginning end will vary with the springiness of the fibers and the use the cord is to undergo. When the wrapping has progressed as far as desired toward the head of the loop, the end of the wrapping cord is stuck through the loop like a thread through the eye of a needle.

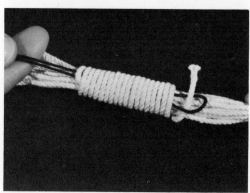

After the loop is threaded, both ends of the looped cord are pulled downward simultaneously. This pulls the loop free of the wrapping and, at the same time, pulls the far end of the wrapping cord down under the wrapping. A little practice with the material will show how tightly a particular fiber may be wrapped and still allow the loop to be pulled out of it.

The ends of yarn at the bottom of Jean Hudson's sleeveless vest (see the chapter on Chinese braids) are finished by wrapping. By taking half of the group of cords to be wrapped from one unit of the braid and half from the adjoining unit of braid, the bottom of the jacket has a more compact finish line than if the cords in each unit had been wrapped together.

There are a number of ways to finish edges and ends in addition to wrapping. What you must decide is whether yarns are to be grouped or whether it is desirable to allow each yarn strand to show as a separate entity.

Small Braids Used as a Finishing Fringe
A wide weaving may have ends braided into a series of small braids. Dixie Mohan wove a purse on a loom, then made the ends into a sampler of many kinds of small braids. The handle is a 3-strand braid, using bundles of yarn as though each bundle were a single strand.

117

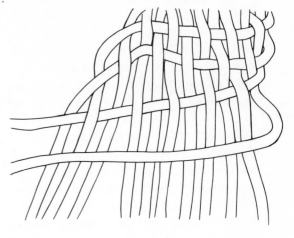

The 4-strand round Indian braid is a most effective way to end a fingerweaving. The long braids which finish the ends of Jo Dendel's afghan are a good example.

The Accumulating Bar

The accumulating bar is a method of gathering all the warp ends into a roll and bringing them together ready for forming into a tassel or other end arrangement. This is particularly useful when points have formed as part of the braiding process. The accumulating bar is made in four steps.

Step 1. The first warp at the edge of the weaving is stretched out across and on top of the other warps. It lies parallel to the last weft. This is called a knot-bearing cord or an anchor cord.

Step 2. The second warp from the edge is led into the first half of a double half hitch made over the anchor cord.

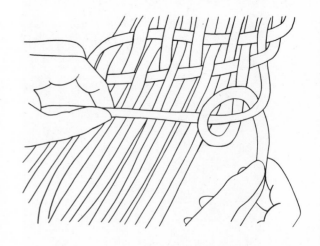

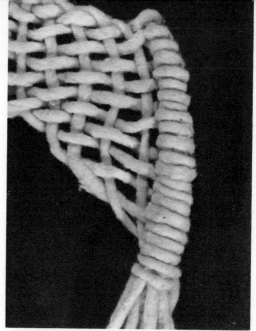

Step 3. The second half of the double half hitch is made.

Step 4. The cord with which the double half hitch was made is placed alongside the anchor cord, making two anchor cords. The third warp from the edge makes a double half hitch over both anchor cords.

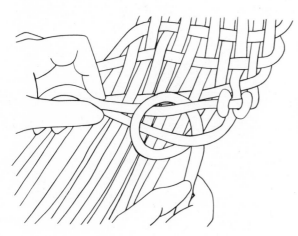

119

Every time a double half hitch is made with it, each warp is gathered up, one at a time, and becomes an addition to the anchor cords. The bundle becomes progressively thicker.

The accumulating bar may progress from right to left or from left to right, depending upon the edge from which one begins. We have shown the bar progressing from right to left.

Jean Hudson used the accumulating bar to good effect at the bottom of her hanging, "Home for Small Treasures."

In the wall hanging, the two groups of yarn emerging from the accumulating bars were joined by figure-of-eight wrapping. (*See overleaf for photo*)

Jean Hudson's Wall Hanging

The Overhand Knot as a Finish

Sometimes an overhand knot tied around two or more other ends and pushed up to the woven edge is sufficient to hold ends in place.

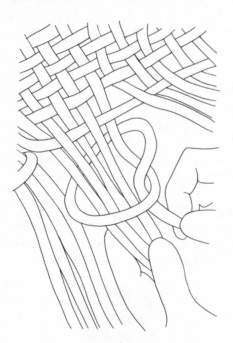

Jean Hudson used this simple finish for the ends of the tie she made for her husband (see color plate #10).

Overhand Knots Used in the Philippine Edge

The Philippine Edge is an elaboration of an overhand knot. It is an attractive finish and a single row of it is usually enough to give a firm edge to a fingerweaving.

One begins work at the left side. Counting in from the left edge, pick up the *third* cord. Take it to the left across the first and the second cords and around behind both of them. Pull the end snugly up to the right between the second and third ends. In other words, wrap the third cord around the first and second cords and bring it to the surface between the second cord and its own beginning.

After the third cord is pulled tight, it drops down in place with the other ends.

In step two, the *fourth* cord from the left edge wraps around the second and third cords in the same way. The fourth cord then drops down into place.

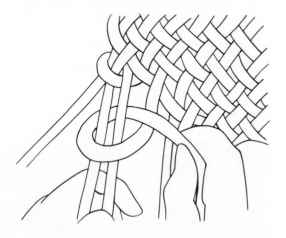

Continue along the edge to be finished, each time picking up a new cord and wrapping it around the two which are immediately at the left. As the finish continues along an edge it takes on the appearance of a pigtail braid.

If two or more rows of Philippine Edge are made, starting from the same left side, the edge will shift to the right. For that reason, the work is turned over on alternate rows when more than one row is desired.

Damascus Edge

An excellent way to knot each strand of yarn at the end of a woven piece is a technique called the Damascus edge, often used by makers of fine rugs. If you look back at the detailed photograph of Mel Kernahan's ruana on page 70, you will see how perfectly this edge finishes off a project.

It is done in two steps—the first step places all the yarns back over the work; the second brings them down again to become a fringe.

Step 1. Pick up the first end on the right side, using the right hand. With the left hand grasping the second end and holding it taut, take the first end over the second and bring it up between them, toward the top of the woven piece.

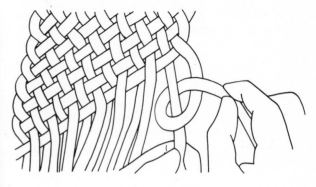

Now hold the second cord in the right hand and the third cord tautly in the left hand and repeat the action, bringing the second cord over the third and up between them. Continue in sequence across the edge, all except the last cord, which has no other cord to go over.

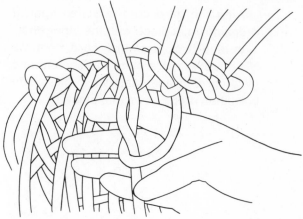

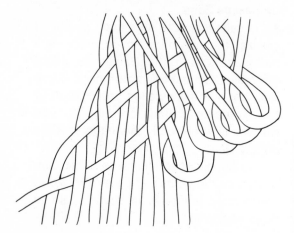

Step 2. Turn the work around so that the edge is at the top and the loose ends are facing down toward you. Take the first cord on the right, the one that had no cord to wrap around on the first row, and wrap it around the second cord and up between the pair as before. As it is wrapped, each cord is brought down where it belongs.

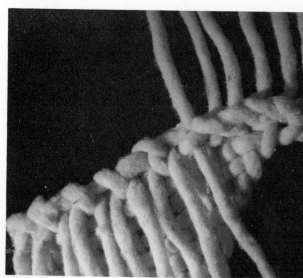

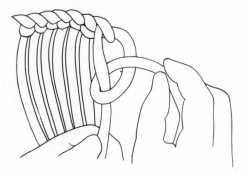

Braiding Down to a Level Edge

Because strands worked by fingers alone weave through one another at an oblique angle, the end of the work is seldom level. In some cases, a slanting edge is desirable but there are times when the finished edge needs to be straight. Here is how to braid down to a level edge, using the Peruvian flat braid as an example. The same method may be used to straighten the edge of any of the braids.

The principle of leveling is that the weft yarn coming from the shorter edge stops before it reaches the longer edge, usually one warp short in each successive row.

When all of the wefts have been stopped at regular intervals, the bottom edge becomes level. Usually the weft yarn stops weaving by one less warp in each successive row.

Finish off the edge by any method you choose.

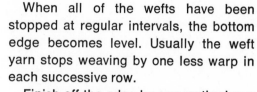

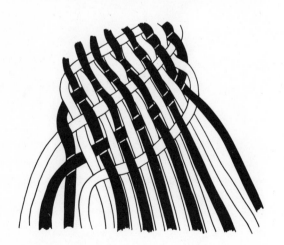

Sources of Supplies

Contessa Yarns
P.O. Box 37
Lebanon, Ct. 06249

Coulter Studios
130 E. 60th Street
New York, N.Y. 10022

Countryside Handweavers
P.O. Box 1743
Estes Park, Co. 80517

Craft Yarns of R.I., Inc.
603 Mineral Spring Ave.
Pawtucket, R.I. 02862

Denwar Craft Studios
236 E. 16th St.
Costa Mesa, Ca. 92627

Lily Mills
Shelby, N.C. 28150

Mexiskeins
Sharon Murfin
P.O. Box 1624
Missoula, Mt. 59801

School Products
312 E. 23rd Street
New York, N.Y. 10010

Tahki Imports
336 West End Avenue
New York, N.Y. 10023

The Yarn Depot
545 Sutter St.
San Francisco, Ca. 94102

Fingerweaving Techniques